IN THE PALACES OF HEAVEN

Christopher Paul Carter

Published by The Fig and The Vine Publishing, LLC

753 Winthrop St.

Mt. Pleasant, SC 29466

thefigandthevinemedia.com

ISBN: 978-0-9883370-7-7

Cover graphic design by: Cristina Young, C Design, Inc.

DEDICATION

Throughout my life, I've had a lot of excellent teachers. Some lived millennia ago, and others continue to impart to me on a daily basis. They include my family, my spiritual mentors, and those who taught me physics and astronomy. To everyone who has taken the time to teach me something, whether you meant to or not, I'd like to dedicate this book to you.

CONTENTS

PREFACE

I like a good adventure. And I have to confess I get excited about maps. Looking at the lay of the land and plotting a course is time well spent for me. Whether it's a road trip across the country or missionary work, I feel like I'm at my best when I'm traveling somewhere and discovering something new. I like learning about it just as much as doing it, which is why I can hardly pass a globe without giving it a spin and looking at some undiscovered land (for me at least) and wondering what it's like to be there.

Astronomy is a favorite hobby of mine for that very reason. When I look through a telescope, I'm seeing all the way to the farthest reaches of everything we think is out there. I find the awesome scale of it beautiful and thought provoking, and even though the view through the telescope is often blurry and faint, I can't help feeling like I've experienced it somehow. Even without a telescope, a good starry night is enough to captivate me for hours. It's like looking out at a celestial ocean that's begging to be explored and navigated. The truth is, however, the stars in the sky are not the farthest things out there. We know that beyond the veil of the sky is something else that mankind and the Bible have defined throughout history as the heavens.

For some years now, the Lord has opened a door for me through His Holy Spirit to experience the heavens, and it has been the greatest adventure of my life. I have taken journeys in the Spirit to the Garden, the throne rooms of heaven, my own heavenly home, and other locations that are still a mystery to me. I've had the privilege of befriending angels and learning how their world works. And although I have loved the adventure and discovery, the whole reason the Lord thrust me into this is so that I would become closer to Him. And that is the ultimate reason I'd like to share all this with you. So, before you jump into the material, let me explain what I hope you get out of this.

*   *   *

Every time I have shared these experiences with people it always seems to build their faith. Hearing about conversations with Jesus in His throne room or how the angels are involved in our lives brings some of the unseen things into earthly reality. That alone can bolster one's faith and I hope these testimonies have that effect on you. Second, I've learned some lessons along the way that are worth sharing. They cover everything from learning about His love and character to the nature of the heavens, themselves. Finally, after reading through the testimonies, you'll be invited to start your own journey into the heavenly places. And I can help you with that, as you will see.

I believe that this is for everyone. And for the record, this didn't happen to me just because I was a super-special Christian and had it all together. In fact, I can assure you that the opposite was true. The point is, experiencing heaven is not for "elite" Christians and everyone else just needs to work on sinning less. Experiencing life in the Spirit is available to all of us; and the practical advice at the end of the book is there to help you get started or further equip you on your journey.

One last note before we get started in earnest. A few years ago I wrote a book entitled *Caught Up in the Spirit: A Journey from Complacency to Glory*. That book recounted my journey from typical, complacent Christianity to the beginning of seeing and walking in the heavenly places. In some ways, *In the Palaces of Heaven* is the sequel to that work. I think it would be helpful to read *Caught Up in the Spirit* first, as it contains a lot of doctrinal background that will not be repeated in detail. Also, much of that book is about getting connected to the Lord's overwhelming love for us, which may be the most important step in experiencing life in the Spirit.

Now if you're ready for an adventure, feel free to jump right into the material. My prayer is that perceiving, and interacting with the heavenly realm will be as normal for you as reading your Bible, and I pray that there will be a whole generation of believers who are as connected and conscious of the heavens as they are the earth.

God speed on your journey.

CHAPTER 1

INTRODUCTION

When you tell someone that you've visited heaven, be prepared to receive some interesting looks. It's not really normal. That doesn't mean that people don't want to believe you, it's just that the material world around us demands all of our attention and has the monopoly on defining what is and is not normal human life. That's not always a good thing. If your attention drifts away from the stoplights, financial demands, and constant barrage of extracurricular activities and media, someone might say you are "out of touch." If this happens when you're in school, you might get called a daydreamer. They might even say your "head is in the clouds." And while all those statements are given to imply that something is wrong with you, I would say just the opposite. I hope your head is in the "clouds of heaven." I hope you do dream during the day and I hope you are "out of touch" with this world and very connected to the heavenly one.

But to the world we live in, trying to see things that are unseen is a waste of time and will supposedly make you unproductive. Like most man-made thought processes, this one just doesn't hold water. Being connected with heaven in a real, discernible way does not leave you unconcerned and irresponsible with the land and people around you. Far from it. There is only one way to be truly connected with the earth, and that is by understanding its connections to heaven. One of the blessings of being a human fashioned in God's image is the ability to perceive and interact with the entire Kingdom, and that means all the realms of heaven as well as the earth.

I've been encouraged these last few years by how many people are talking about their heavenly encounters and how many books are written about this topic. You may call a recent best-selling book that covers this subject called *Heaven is So Real* by Choo Thomas. Or *Heaven Is for Real: A Little Boy's Astounding Story of His Trip to Heaven and Back* by Todd Burpo and Lynn Vincent, or *The Boy Who Came Back from Heaven* by Mark and Alex Malarkey. These are just a few recent books that describe visits to heaven from both near-death (or return from death might be a better term) and "visitations in the spirit" experiences. I don't think this is just a fad that will blow over in a couple of years. An interest in what goes on in the unseen realms is here to stay, partly because it's simply just time for it. I believe God has ordained this season of human — more specifically Christian — history to restore one more thing that had been lost in the Garden of Eden and won back at the cross. So even though it still may not be normal, it is definitely gaining some ground.

We all could use a little scriptural background so that these "out of this world" experiences don't get labeled as unbiblical. First of all, there are the classic examples of Enoch and Elijah. When it comes to having a heavenly experience, these guys might set the standard. After all, they visited heaven and never came back! That's a pretty neat feat, skipping out on death and entering the heavenly realm with no dead body left behind. But we might be able to learn a little more from those who experienced that other dimension while their bodies were still firmly planted on earth.

Two well-known prophets, Isaiah and Ezekiel, both had an experience in which the veil between the earthly and the heavenly was pulled back for a moment. Both of these men describe in detail what they saw of God's throne and the various spiritual creatures surrounding it. Isaiah's testimony is written in *Isaiah*, chapter 6, while Ezekiel's encounter is recorded at the very start of his book in the Bible. I'd recommend reading these accounts on your own; they are awe-inspiring to say the least. What's important, though, is that they didn't have to go somewhere in their physical bodies to perceive the heavenly realm. Isaiah was in the temple and Ezekiel was down by a river. And in both cases, that wafer-thin barrier between dimensions was pulled back so that the observer could see and interact with heaven without his body leaving the earth.

Now, here is one of my all time favorites. It's the story of the prophet Elisha and his servant. As it goes in the story, the King of Aram was not happy with Elisha and came with his army to get him. Here is the account in *2 Kings 15-17*:

> *Now when the attendant of the man of God had risen early and gone out, behold, an army with horses and chariots was circling the city. And his servant said to him, "Alas, my master! What shall we do?" So he answered, "Do not fear, for those who are with us are more than those who are with them." Then Elisha prayed and said, "O Lord, I pray, open his eyes that he may see." And the Lord opened the servant's eyes and he saw; and behold, the mountain was full of horses and chariots of fire all around Elisha.*

What's cool about this story is that Elisha didn't have

to pray for his own eyes to be opened. The implication is that he was already seeing the chariots of fire, and it must have been somewhat normal to him because he didn't wake up and say to his servant, "Hey, do you see all those angelic warriors, too?" Be honest, wouldn't you shout and make sure you hadn't gone off the deep end if you suddenly started seeing vast numbers of spiritual beings? Elisha didn't do any of that. His lack of surprise should tell us that it was normal and part of every-day life. So normal, in fact, that he didn't mention what he saw until it became important for his servant to see it as well.

This is the same kind of experience that Isaiah and Ezekiel had. They were on the earth in their bodies and were certainly aware of their earthly surroundings; but they were perceiving the heavenly dimension at the same time. Even if they had to take time out to close their eyes and focus in order to look into the spiritual realm, they didn't have to leave earth to do it. They could see heavenly things from right where they were. That's important for this reason: If you don't have to "go" somewhere via a near-death experience or an actual trip to heaven (like Enoch and Elijah) in order to see what's in the heavenly places, then that's one less mental hurdle we have to jump over in order to have our eyes opened like Elisha's servant.

That reminds me of another Biblical story about seeing heavenly things. The Apostle Paul had an experience he didn't talk about too much, but here is his mention of it:

> Boasting is necessary, though it is not profitable; but I will go on to visions and revelations of the Lord. I know a man in Christ who fourteen years ago—whether in the body I do not know, or out of the body I do not know, God knows—such a

man was caught up to the third heaven. And I know how such a man—whether in the body or apart from the body I do not know, God knows—was caught up into Paradise and heard inexpressible words, which a man is not permitted to speak. (2 Corinthians 12: 1-5)

Paul didn't give us a lot of details and he did everything he could to take the focus of this story off of himself. However, he clearly had a heavenly experience, and it left an unmistakable impression on his message to the church. Look at some of his advice and prayers in his letters to Christians.

For momentary, light affliction is producing for us an eternal weight of glory far beyond all comparison, while we look not at the things which are seen, but at the things which are not seen; for the things which are seen are temporal, but the things which are not seen are eternal. (2 Corinthians 4: 17-18)

I pray that the eyes of your heart may be enlightened, so that you will know what is the hope of His calling, what are the riches of the glory of His inheritance in the saints, and what is the surpassing greatness of His power toward us who believe. (Ephesians 1: 18-19)

We could make a case that whatever Paul saw (and however he saw it) left him with the impression that what was going on in heaven was way more important, or to use his word, eternal, than what could be observed on the earth. In the second quote you can hear the same prayer that Elisha prayed over his servant, "Lord, open their eyes!" So, to recap the information so far, here are the points I'm making:

- People seeing and interacting with the heavenly realm is Biblical.
- There are biblical examples of people seeing into the heavens without leaving earth.
- It was so normal to Elisha that he wasn't caught by surprise.
- It's normal enough that Paul encourages the entire Christian church to do it.

If we can grasp all of that, we'll be heading in the right direction for sure; but there is still one more example that sheds a lot of light on all this. It's the life and testimony of John the Apostle. He left us two very important pieces of the puzzle, one way more obvious than the other. The one that jumps out is our last book in the Bible called *Revelation*. The whole thing is an account of one of John's journeys into the heavens, and it will help us with the protocols we will discuss in later chapters. The second (less noticeable) testimony comes in the gospel he penned. For a full explanation you might want to read the section in *Caught Up in the Spirit* that deals with John at the Last Supper, but let's highlight at least one point: While they were sitting around the table and enjoying a very intimate moment with the Lord, Jesus says something very alarming:

> *But because I have said these things to you, sorrow has filled your heart. Nevertheless I tell you the truth. It is to your advantage that I go away; for if I do not go away, the Helper will not*

come to you; but if I depart, I will send Him to you. (John 16: 6-7 NKJV)

This may be one of the best prophecies about the forthcoming Holy Spirit. If the disciples were wondering what it would be like when "the Helper" comes, the answer from Jesus is that it would be, to paraphrase and summarize, "Better than this!" That's what Jesus means when He says, "It is to your advantage that I go…" Sitting with Jesus at the table and having a two- way conversation sounds great, but the Holy Spirit is even better than that!

I often ask people to consider this choice: Would you choose a personal, one-on-one conversation with Jesus at your kitchen table, where you are eating the same food and talking with him like you would your earthly friends (which is what the disciples were doing)? Or would you take your present relationship with Him through the Holy Spirit? Most people predictably choose the first one — and why not? Most of us are straining through our prayer times and just trying to stay awake in church, so an actual, physical experience of having a conversation with the Lord at a table sounds pretty good. But, that choice is a great indicator that we haven't received the full blessing of the Holy Spirit. Because the Helper is supposed to be better than that, remember?

Well, we don't have to wonder if the advent of the Holy Spirit really trumped the intimacy and friendship they experienced at the Last Supper or not, we can read all about it. The proof in the pudding comes from John's later revelation. The whole final book of the Bible is one long journey into the heavenly places — and guess what makes it all possible? The Holy Spirit. When the Helper was poured out, it gave the disciples access to an intimacy with God that they hadn't even dreamed about. Before, they sat at the table with Him. After Pentecost, they sat in the heavenly places with Him, too.

> *But God, being rich in mercy, because of His great love with which He loved us, even when we were dead in our transgressions, made us alive together with Christ (by grace you have been saved), 6 and raised us up with Him, and seated us with Him in the heavenly places in Christ Jesus. (Ephesians 2:4-6)*

Their intimacy with God didn't take a hit when Jesus left — it got an upgrade! So while we are thinking about and longing for a conversation with Jesus around a table, we might be missing out on something categorically better. It's something that not only provides space for those two-way talks like you have with your earthly friends, but also brings you into His presence in ways that this earthly dimension doesn't have room for yet.

John doesn't leave us hanging about how the Holy Spirit makes all of this possible, either. In the very first verses of *Revelation*, he gives us that second piece of the puzzle.

> *I, John, your brother and fellow partaker in the tribulation and kingdom and perseverance which are in Jesus, was on the island called Patmos because of the word of God and the testimony of Jesus. 10 I was in the Spirit on the Lord's day... (Revelation 1: 9-10)*

John's body was on the Isle of Patmos, but his persona (for lack of a better term) was "in the Spirit." Remember our examples of people experiencing the heavens from where they were sitting? This is that same kind of encounter. John wrote a whole book based on this one experience in the Spirit, and from start to finish it is a heavenly journey. John speaks with the Lord, with elders, and with angels; he gets taken to various places to see what's coming on the earth, and — last but not least — he visits the New Jerusalem, that glorious, golden city. And here is the best part: It was normal.

When John says that he was "in the Spirit," he was not making a radical statement. In fact there are many, many uses of that phrase after the coming of the Helper in *Acts, chapter 2*. Maybe the best indicator that being in the Spirit was commonplace is that nobody feels obligated to explain what it means. John says it in passing; like it's what he does on most days, but on that particular day he got a lot of prophetic material that he was instructed to share with the church. In other words, being "in the Spirit" wasn't the special part. The special part was what was shared with him at that time while he was "in the Spirit" — because it needed to be read by everyone. It's like this: If I tell you that I wore blue jeans yesterday, I would not feel obligated to explain what blue jeans are; everyone already knows. So John wasn't being mystical about his experience; he was communicating it in terms that were well understood, and he wasn't the only one to do that. The Apostle Paul says something similar that we will look at later.

It's easy to think that Elisha, Isaiah, and Ezekiel saw what they did because they had jobs that required some extra help from heaven, and that would be true. John, however, experienced what he did because of a gift that was poured out on everyone who believed in Jesus. This wasn't very common in the times of the Old Testament, and only a handful of prophets had stories to tell like this. But in John's day everything had changed. The ability to perceive the heavens, and converse with Jesus in that environment was possible for everyone through the Holy Spirit. Remember Jesus' words (and I'm paraphrasing here), "When I leave, there is something better coming!"

Today, when people ask me how I see the heavenly places or how I take part in a conversation with Jesus or His ministering spirits, I answer like this: I'm doing it "in the Spirit." I'm not doing anything that John wasn't doing on the Isle of Patmos. As I mentioned before, I believe this function of Christian life is now being restored, and most of our ministry is helping people discover this. So, as we walk through the testimonies starting in this next chapter, please keep two things in mind. First, while this may not be normal to the world around us, it is certainly Biblical. Second, contrary to the common warning, "trained professional, do not try this at home," please do just the opposite. Try this at home! Read through the testimonies in these chapters and then start your own journey in the Spirit. Before it's all said and done, I'll give you some pointers and walk you through how to get started. For now, I'll tell you how it started with me.

Chapter 2

The Invitation

It all started in a prison cell. Thankfully, I don't mean that in earthly terms. In my body, I was sitting in a living room, in a nice comfortable chair, having a scheduled prayer time. But when I opened my heart to the Lord and asked Him to show me whatever He liked, I immediately saw prison bars. It wasn't a flash of a picture that faded away, either. It lasted. It seemed permanent and it wasn't much work at all to keep watching this scene like I would a movie. I was having an experience in the Spirit, although I didn't quite know it yet. However, the environment I began to see wasn't immediately encouraging, and if I had wanted to, I'm sure I could have opened my earthly, biological eyes and seen the comforting confines of the living room in which I was praying. But what I really wanted to know was why I was in a prison cell. So I kept looking.

The prison cell was dark and small. I was standing next to the cell door and holding onto the bars. If that sounds like a pretty sad scene to you, rest assured it was to me as well. It was restrictive and confining. It was all the things a prison cell is supposed to make you feel. Then there was a ray of hope. Jesus walked towards the barred door and held up a key. In that moment, when I asked myself why I was in that prison to begin with, my answer was simple. I did not feel good enough for Jesus. I never thought I would be worthy of His company or favor. I never

15

thought He would be overwhelmingly good to me. That belief — or rather that unbelief — is what defined my confinement.

It was so comforting to have Jesus there, even though I was imprisoned. In fact, it was just plain great to see Jesus. It was the longest I had ever really seen Him and it was easy to focus on Him and let the details of his face, clothing, and posture become clearer. Then, He freed me. He took the key and opened the door and walked me out of that dark cell. If someone were looking at me in my body, sitting in the reclining chair, they would have thought nothing abnormal was happening. I looked like a man in prayer, with maybe a few small tears starting to roll down my cheeks. But inside myself I was in another world. I came out of the cell with Jesus and walked with him for a while, amazed that this "movie" kept going. Eventually, He brought me to a rectangular wooden table and sat me down. I sat on one end while He sat at the other end, the head of the table, in a high-backed chair. I couldn't help noticing that sitting at the table on both sides were what looked like people. This was definitely unexpected.

The one sitting to my immediate right looked like a man, but one I didn't recognize. I couldn't help asking, "Who are you?" The man responded to me, "I'm David." Now, in moments like these, when you are way out of your comfort zone, you respond to the unexpected in humorous ways. Think about Peter on the Mount of Transfiguration. Jesus, Moses and Elijah show up in glorified form and Peter has a bit of a hard time processing the whole scene:

And while He was praying, the appearance of His face became different, and His clothing became white and gleaming. And

*behold, two men were talking with Him; and they were Moses
and Elijah, who, appearing in glory, were speaking of His
departure which He was about to accomplish at Jerusalem.
Now Peter and his companions had been overcome with sleep;
but when they were fully awake, they saw His glory and the two
men standing with Him. And as these were leaving Him, Peter
said to Jesus, "Master, it is good for us to be here; let us make
three tabernacles: one for You, and one for Moses, and one for
Elijah"— not realizing what he was saying. (Luke 9:29-33)*

In my case, when the man next to me said he was David, I started thinking about all the "Davids" I knew and why one of them
would be sitting at that table with me. The probable identity of
this "David" took me a few moments because it seemed so un-
believable. So I asked, "Which David are you?" He replied with
a big smile and almost playful tone, "I'm David from the Bible!"

I just sat there staring at him because I didn't know
what else to do, or what the appropriate response to meeting
King David in the Spirit is supposed to be. There isn't exactly
a manual on this. But before long, he looked at me with a deep
gaze and said pleadingly, "Just worship Him." Those were the
words that snapped me out of my shocked paralysis, and suddenly I could discern the identity of everyone sitting around
that table. One by one I looked at each person as he gave me
a one-sentence encouragement like David had done. To the
right of David sat Moses. Next to him was Elijah and Elisha.
Then at the head of table I looked again at the seated figure of
Jesus. He wore a smile so big and enthusiastic. It was a smile
that said, "I've waited and waited for this day! You had no
idea the riches and blessings I have wanted to release to you!"

On the left side of the table next to Jesus sat Isaiah, then Ezekiel, then Matthew. Paul and John were the last two sitting to my left. As they spoke to me, the emotions became overwhelming. In the Spirit, I was sitting at the table mesmerized by this company. In my body, the weeping started and never stopped until this whole journey came to a close some three hours later. Here is the order in which they spoke and what they had to say:

David: Just worship Him.

Moses: Never underestimate Him.

Elijah: Always stay close to Him.

Elisha: Just live in His abundance.

Isaiah: Keep looking ahead.

Ezekiel: Live in His glory.

Matthew: Don't be afraid to write.

Paul: Never stop looking at Jesus.

John: All you need is love.

This was the moment when I first had the conscious thought that I was in actually in the Spirit. Up until this meeting, it just felt like a vision that lasted a really long time. But when Moses told me not to underestimate the Lord, I felt like I was getting a life lesson from the actual man who lived it. It was as if Moses was telling me, "Christopher, this is what I learned from my time on earth... Don't underestimate the Lord." These were real, living men with real stories to tell. They spoke in voices that were different from one another, and not all of their advice was predictable. Matthew's words to me were like a shockwave. Not only were they extremely timely, as I was in the middle of writing *Caught Up in the Spirit*, but they were also so personal to him. Sometimes it's hard to imagine the twelve apostles as men like us, but in that moment I knew that Matthew had to face his own fears in order to write down the gospel. From one writer to another, that was welcome encouragement.

Whenever I have told this story, it's always John's advice that gets a laugh. Many people have come up to me suggesting that it was the famous Beatle, John Lennon who sat at the table. Of course that wasn't the case, but John did say, "All you need is love," with a bit of a knowing grin. So from David to John, as they went around the table giving their statements, I sat there soaking it all in. Later that day I reflected on this table meeting and found a lot of common ground with the following scripture:

> *Therefore, since we are surrounded by such a great cloud of witnesses, let us throw off everything that hinders and the sin that so easily entangles. And let us run with perseverance the race marked out for us, fixing our eyes on Jesus, the pioneer and perfecter of faith. (Hebrews 12:1-2)*

The words of advice from those witnesses gave me courage and confidence — and it was the perfect preamble to what came next. Jesus got up from the table and walked me to a bright, golden door. I stood there with Him on one side and an angel on the other. I was also aware in this moment that I looked different. I was dressed in a pure white and blue robe that had the finest gold embroidery. Before I opened the door, I took one last look around. I looked back at the table of witnesses. I looked back at the prison cell. Something in me knew the next step across this threshold was defining. From the time I sat down at the table, to the moment before we walked through that golden door, the realization was setting in that even though my body was still sitting in a soft chair on earth, my persona was somewhere else. I was there, with Jesus and the angel, in the Spirit.

We stepped through that door and right into the cosmos. The stars and galaxies hung around me and I floated up into the firmament holding tightly to Jesus' hand. I watched him make stars and planets out of his bare hands and scatter them out into the universe. As we seemed to float on together, He brought me to another table. This one, however, was just for the two of us. I sat next to Him and saw on a piece of paper the words being written:

THE ONLY WAY TO BELIEVE IS TO PUT ALL OF YOUR TRUST IN ME.

As I sat next to Him at the table, I looked at Him for a long moment. Nothing was being said; I just looked at Him. I saw His eyes, which were more than just striking; they were my undoing. In my body, the heaves and tears came like a flood, and in the Spirit, I felt like I was falling into His eyes. It was like falling into a well of love and acceptance that had no end. Until that moment, I don't know if I had ever felt 100% loved and accepted in my whole life.

Peace… that is the only word I know to describe my state of being in that moment. I had stopped seeing or hearing anything while I just rested in His love and acceptance. And when I felt like I had fallen to the end of it (if that were possible), I found myself standing in front of a pool of crystal clear water. On the other side of that pool was a throne, and sitting on the throne was the Father. I walked up the steps leading to the throne. I took in as much of His Presence as I could. To me, He looked like all of the aspects of creation encapsulated in a vaguely human form. Energy seemed to swirl around His seated figure. He was awesome, yet still approachable, and I did not feel like I needed an invitation to walk up those stairs to His throne. It all seemed to make sense. Jesus' overwhelming love had brought me here and I wasn't afraid to draw closer to see. As I walked up the steps, I got hit with another round of pure love and acceptance. Each step brought it on with more intensity until I stood at the top facing Him.

If there has ever been a defining moment of my life, this was it. The Father stood up off of His throne and motioned to the side with His hand. A door opened up into a lush green garden that was bursting with life. He then looked at me and said, "You can come here and walk and talk with Me as often as you like."

After He gave that invitation, I came back to earth. My body was still in the chair, my shirt was soaked with tears, and my spirit had just been on an inaugural journey. I was very unproductive the rest of the day, and most of the time I just wondered aloud at what had happened. I needed about twenty-four hours to take it all in, but the invitation that seemed to be the crux of the whole experience called to me. That experience was by far the most amazing thing that had ever happened to me, and to be promised access to that realm as often as I wanted to go seemed downright surreal.

And, it was all so easy. I don't think I can stress enough how much being in the Spirit is a work of the Holy Spirit and not a result of our efforts. I had a lot of grace that first day to focus on what I was seeing with the eyes of my heart; but even after that day, it never became a matter of effort or straining. That is not to say, however, that it always felt easy; but we will get to that later. For now, I just want to highlight what Jesus wrote on that piece of paper as we sat together in the cosmos.

THE ONLY WAY TO BELIEVE IS TO PUT ALL OF YOUR TRUST IN ME..

He made it all about Him. He just wanted me to rest in the work that He had done, and to know that He provided a way for me to know Him in the Spirit. So armed only with that confidence, I went to my office the next day intending to put the promise to the test. What happened was more than just the fulfillment of the Father's words; it was an introduction into a whole other realm.

By the way, if you're wondering if I understood everything that was happening to me that day, I most certainly did not! I had tons of questions. Was it theologically correct to interact with angels? Was it heresy to see and receive encouragement from people that lived thousands of years ago? Was this all just my imagination? As I mentioned before, I think it is very important to have some scriptural backup to our experiences. Seeing how something is Biblical and well within God's character gives us confidence to keep going. In the chapters to come, I will explain it to you as the Lord taught it to me — and we will hit on every one of those normal areas of caution. If you're like me and want to make sure you're not breaking any rules, just hang in there for a little bit. Interspersed in the journeys to the heavenly places were life lessons and scriptural reminders that not only put me at ease, but also made me realize this kind of experience wasn't just allowed. It was promised.

CHAPTER 3

THE GARDEN

The very next day I planned to put the Father's promise to the test. I drove to my office and got settled in a quiet environment. Sitting on the floor with my eyes closed, I uttered a little prayer in the hope of not being disappointed. When I opened the eyes of my heart, I was right back where I left off the previous day. I was standing in front of a white, marble throne, and the Father was standing and motioning to an open door. I could still see past that door into a lush, green environment that I just instinctually knew was The Garden.

There must be something deep, deep down in our spiritual DNA that longs for the first environment man ever knew. It isn't just about nice flowers or manicured trees; it's about an all-natural, perfectly comfortable, expertly managed, and totally peaceful place that just feels right. I looked into that garden and had a sense that I belong there and that if the earth were perfect, it might look something like that. The Father then took my hand and walked me through that door, and there we stood in that bright, green land. It was like I had only seen the world in black and white; and now I could finally see in true colors. I could see the trees and each individual leaf in detail. I could see the blue sky. I could see the short grass under my feet, and I could see Him. He didn't look like He did the day before, as the cosmic elements all wrapped up into one body.

He looked more normal. His clothes were deep reds and golds. He had a discernible face and expression, and I could see a smile inside His beard. This wasn't just an all-powerful being that was overwhelmingly good and altruistic; this was my Dad.

I held His hand as we took those first steps in the garden together. The first thing I noticed were how all the trees and various plants seemed to respond to His presence. There was so much life in this garden to begin with, as if all the flora and fauna let off a little bit of a glow. But when the Father walked by a plant, the leaves seemed to reach out to Him. If it were possible, it looked like they came to life even more just because He walked by. I wasn't all that different than these leaves, either. I think if you have life in you, it swells up like a wave when you are in His presence, and the life in me was expanding and growing in every step. The next thing I noticed was the people walking about, some alone and others in pairs. Now, I will say this without blushing: everyone was naked. I don't mean that in a biological sense, although that was also true. It was a shame-free environment, which was a result of perfect and unhindered life. Even though I knew everyone was naked, I just didn't think anything of it. The glory coming off each person was what I noticed.

We walked over to a tree where I could see a man sitting in the shade. He sat in front of a delicate, gold easel, and I watched him draw and design things for a few moments. He drew out sketches of plants and houses and as I looked over his shoulder, I knew this wasn't just an artist practicing his drawing technique. There was a sense of creation about it, like what he drew on the paper would become reality when he finished. And he seemed so unhurried. The patience and contentment to just sit and draw until his heart was content mesmerized me. I looked back at the Father and asked who he was. If you recall from my first journey in the Spirit, I had met some of the "cloud of witnesses." Was this person another Biblical saint with an encouraging word? The Father told me to go look at him. So, walking around to the side, I looked at his face and saw my own! I froze. This wasn't a random person; it was me. I was there, walking in the garden for the first time, and yet there I was in the garden, naked and glorious and perfect... already. That completed version of me smiled knowingly and I had to ask the Father for an explanation before my brain exploded.

The Father is the master of time. To Him, it is just another dimension that we move in. So He allowed me to see into the future all the way to the New Heavens and New Earth when all things are completed, including me. What makes this so interesting to a Physics nut like myself is that one day I will be sitting under that tree designing/creating something and I'll remember when my Dad brought me there in the Spirit before I received my eternal body! Now, if that doesn't make your head spin with its quantum ramifications, I don't know what will. In the years since these inaugural visits in the Spirit, this has happened a few times. On one occasion, the Lord let the "future me" tell me some encouraging words about the years to come. Yes, it's possible to send messages back through time when your Dad is the one who created that dimension.

From there, we continued to walk through the Garden to a secluded spot, away from the other people milling about. It looked like a little hidden corner with green vines growing all around. Just like a Dad telling His son a story He proceeded to tell me about my birth and the state of the world and my family when I was born. Then he brought up something that had been a struggle to me for years. He said, "Christopher, you are very analytical and very emotional." I responded, "I know! That's why I feel so weird all the time. It's like oil and water in the same vessel; they don't mix very well." And that was true. I often wondered what was wrong with me because I had two very different processes working in my soul all the time. Then the Father looked at me with a loving expression and said, "You are passionately analytical. Don't feel discouraged about that. Everyone on the earth is displaying different parts of My whole personality." That was liberating. Sometimes it's hard to tell if God got it right or made huge mistakes in the way He designed us. Hearing from my Father's mouth that my personality had the given name "passionately analytical" and that it was by design made me feel normal and on-purpose.

The first day in the Garden had a couple more important points. First, my interaction with the Father could be described as a two-way conversation in which all of my senses were working, albeit in another realm. If you will hearken back to our discussion of Jesus' promise at the Last Supper that something better was coming than sitting at the table with Him, well, this was the first day I might have known what Jesus was talking about. I knew I had a Father in Heaven, but to be able to walk and talk with Him and learn things about myself I never knew was a dream come true. Second, the Garden of Eden was a place of intimacy with God. It was perfect communion before the taint of sin entered the picture. The Father chose that place for our first talk, person to person. The message to me was that experiencing the Lord in the Spirit is all about a restored intimacy with Him. Finally, and I didn't know this then, but walking in the heavenly places was going to reveal to me who I really was.

If you noticed, the first thing the Father took me to see was myself. We will build on that issue a lot in this book, because living in the Holy Spirit will show you that the biological shell you are used to seeing is not who you are. It is just that — the biology that surrounds your spirit. And it is destined to be replaced by something greater and incorruptible. In order to see who you are and how God really designed you, you need to look in the Spirit. You are far brighter and more perfectly made than you ever realized. To see that in the scriptures, take a look at this statement from the Apostle Paul:

> *Therefore, from now on we recognize no one according to the flesh; even though we have known Christ according to the flesh, yet now we know Him in this way no longer. Therefore if anyone is in Chirst, he is a new creature; the old things passed aways; behold, new things have come. (2 Corinthians 5: 16-17)*

CHAPTER 4

MY FIRST DAY OF SCHOOL

The first couple of weeks I made time almost everyday to go up to the heavens and see what my Lord had for me, and most of that time was spent in the Garden. A friend of mine asked me about the frequency of my visits in those days, and when I told him that I did this "most days" he was shocked. He told me that if heaven were available to him he would be going everyday — for sure. What he didn't know is that in the beginning it took some getting used to. There where days when I was so shocked to have spent time walking with my Lord in the heavenly places that I just took a break for a few days to process the experience. Also, learning to use my internal, spiritual eyes (and other senses) was an endurance exercise. Even though the Lord never made it hard, my physical body would be worn out after thirty minutes of walking in the Spirit. However, from one week to the next, that time got longer and longer.

Just a quick note for those of you willing to try on your own: it takes practice. I tell folks to think of your spiritual eyes like a muscle that has atrophied from lack of use. The muscle has always been there, but it will take some rehab to get it back into shape before it can lift something. For some people, this could take years (it did with me). But, just like any muscle, the more you work it, the stronger it gets. And don't be discouraged at the "it could take years" statement. I am referring to the more complete experience of it, so don't feel that it will take years before you can see anything — that's not the case at all.

Part of the "rehab" for me was time in the heavenly school — and I'm not ashamed to say that my education in the heavens started with the elementary subjects of reading and writing. To show you what I mean, one day I walked with Jesus in the Garden to a little clearing with desks set out in ordered rows. It looked like a small outdoor classroom. When I sat down, the Lord put a book in front of me and opened it up. It was a Bible, and I was instantly drawn to a certain part of the page while Jesus encouraged me to read. This took some prodding from Him because I was unsure about how to do that; I was afraid I might read something and be totally wrong about it. For instance, what if I tried to read scripture in the Spirit and ended up seeing a recipe for macaroni and cheese? I think that would have seriously dampened my trust in the Holy Spirit. However, Jesus' gentle encouragement was enough for me to give it a try. So I started reading aloud what I saw.

It turned out to be the parable of the mustard seed, which I didn't know from memory at all. But, I made sure to sound it out exactly as it looked on the page. I'm sure you can guess that as soon as I was done praying and opened my earthly eyes, I checked my physical Bible to see if I had read it correctly. It was the same, word for word. That was the first time I had read anything in the Spirit, and I'm thankful it was something I could cross-reference in the earthly realm. These days, reading in the heavens has become a weekly occurrence, so the Lord made sure to set that foundation early. During the training time, He primarily used the scriptures to encourage cross checking and to build my trust.

Here's another reading that stands out to me. I was looking at the Bible in the Spirit and could clearly see *Exodus 26* at the top of the page. I really don't have that book committed to heart, so I knew it would be a real test. I started reading paragraphs that were all about the tabernacle, but specifically about the design of the curtains that were hung around the perimeter. I thought it was such an obscure thing to read about on earth, much less in the heavenly places with Jesus. Just like the first instance I shared with you, I couldn't wait to get to my physical Bible and see what was in *Exodus 26*. Of course it was all the same as I had seen in the spirit... go look for yourself sometime. To this day, I haven't gotten anything more out of that reading other than a faith building exercise. The Lord never expounded on the symbolism in the design and pattern of the curtains or any other part of that chapter. I think He simply used it to show me I could read scriptures without having any knowledge — at all — of the passage beforehand. That brings me to two points:

First, a wonderful way to direct your scripture reading is to see what passages Jesus and the angels are highlighting that day or week for you. There have been many occasions in the past years where they have given me a daily reading or something to focus on for a whole month and it has been life changing. Second, what if you want to read a Bible and there aren't any around? Or, what if we live in a time and place when Bibles are regularly confiscated, God forbid? The answer is both radical and immediately accessible. Start reading the Bible in the Spirit right now. You can learn how to do it now in times of peace and plenty because someday it just might be a skill you are thankful you have. When you think about it, it makes perfect sense. Why wouldn't there be a copy of the law, prophets, psalms, gospels, and letters in the heavenly places? Since we have ready access there, why can't we read with Jesus in that environment? Also, since there is never any persecution in the heavenly palaces of the Lord, I can promise you that the Bible you read there can never be taken from you.

After reading the scriptures in the Spirit, and building up my trust in reading anything in that realm, the Lord let me read some other books as well. One day we walked to a large clearing in the Garden. Imagine a tree-lined grassy field in the shape of a circle, with just a few shady trees spread out in the clearing. The center of the field was a little lower than the perimeter, giving it a slight concave look. In a moment of awareness I realized I was carrying a satchel of books, and then I also noticed I wasn't the only one there. All around the field were other people sitting by themselves. Some sat under the trees, some in the open sunshine. Jesus walked to the center of the clearing and started teaching, and the concave nature of the clearing had the feel of a gently sloped outdoor amphitheater.

It was like the first day at school. I didn't quite know what to do so I watched the other kids in my class. Everyone listened to Him intently while taking some notes or thumbing through a book. So, I picked my spot under a tree and listened in. I realized Jesus was talking to each of us individually at the same time, about different subjects. We all heard him teaching us as if we were the only ones there. Before I go into what I learned that day, I have to share another "brain explosion" moment. I wondered as I looked at the men and women sitting to my right and left, if we were from different places on earth, but all in the Spirit at the same time? Did Jesus just happen to bring us to class that day? Would I ever meet any of these people on the earth, or just in this heavenly Garden?

The first subject we talked about that day was worship. On my lap I held a book called *Praiseology*, which — you guessed it — means "the study of praise." "How funny," I thought as I opened it up and listened to the lesson. He pointed my attention to the first page where I read about the woman at the well in the gospel of *John*. Here is a snippet of their interaction.

> *The woman said to Him, "Sir, I perceive that You are a prophet. Our fathers worshiped in this mountain, and you people say that in Jerusalem is the place where men ought to worship." Jesus said to her, "Woman, believe Me, an hour is coming when neither in this mountain nor in Jerusalem will you worship the Father. You worship what you do not know; we worship what we know, for salvation is from the Jews. But an hour is coming, and now is, when the true worshipers will worship the Father in spirit and truth; for such people the Father seeks to be His worshipers. (John 4: 19-23)*

Right off the bat we were reading about worship, and the first thing I had to ask was, "How do you worship in the Spirit?" Jesus started by saying this: "When you come together to worship, I don't want you to start your time by trying to give to Me, I want it to start with Me giving to you." He then went on to say, "I want to the be the One who starts the whole worship process, the One who primes the pump, so that I can be preeminent in everything." Jesus was quoting a verse in *Colossians* about how He has the first place in all things (*Colossians 1:18*). He then went on to say that worship is more about receiving than giving, and He painted a picture of people coming togeth-er with hands outstretched, ready to receive the riches from His heavens before they tried to give Him one thing in return.

Before I could repeat my original question, He said to me, "Receiving everything from Me freely, as you are do-ing right now, is worshiping Me in the Spirit." That state-ment has forever changed my impression of what it means to worship Him in spirit and in truth. On the one hand, it means we can worship Him in the heavenly realms as we do on the earth. It also changes what worship looks like when it becomes a matter of receiving and not giving.

I couldn't resist looking at some of the other books in my satchel. I pulled out a nice blue covered book that was titled, *Structure and Building Blocks of the Kingdom.* The Lord had me at the word "structure." I love structures, and it doesn't matter if it's the structure of the cosmos, atmosphere, or the anatomy of a dragonfly; I am just amazed at how God put things to-gether. So, I had to take a peak inside this book, even though I was nearing the end of my endurance to hang around up there. The first chapter was called, "The fundamental building block of the Kingdom," and I looked at the diagram under the title.

It was a picture of a circular stadium, and it seemed to come to life as I watched it. In the center of the stadium, at ground level, was one person walking in the Garden. The lush trees were all around them and the whole Garden "bubble" there in the center seemed to glow with God's glory. People were sitting in the stands of the stadium and milling about. Occasionally, a person would get up and go down to the center and enter the Garden. Just like the people already in there, they would start to glow with the glory of the Lord. While some stayed in there the whole time, others walked back out to sit in the stands again. I even saw some who walked back out tell others sitting near them about what they saw. At the very top of the stands was a walkway that encircled the whole stadium. From that walkway people looked down into the stands and the Garden and out into the world outside of the stadium.

I looked up from the page and Jesus started teaching about what I just read. He said, "The most fundamental element in the Kingdom is one person experiencing the intimacy of the Garden. When they discover that, the Garden starts to exist all around them. People can enter the Garden as a group or one at a time. Once the Garden is present in someone's life, others will come in and find rest. Sometimes they stay, causing the Garden to grow around them, and sometimes they go back out for a season. Others will sit around and watch the life in the Garden, but not take the step to enter it. They learn from watching the others but never experience it for themselves. Still others watch from afar, keeping one eye on the outside world and one eye on the Garden."

As I mentioned in the previous chapter, there is a strong connection between spending time with God in the Garden and knowing who you really are. That's because the more time you spend in that perfect, lush environment, the more you start to feel like Adam, and Adam knew who He was and what God had made Him to do. He was created to rule and have dominion in the Garden; he was made to "keep it" (*Genesis 2: 15*). However, it is really hard to feel like a ruler when you don't know who you are. If Adam had never known his unhindered connection to the Lord, he might have felt totally inadequate for the job at hand. Here is a story that illustrates this very point.

The King of a certain country had a son. This son was captured by the King's enemies while still an infant, and grew up as a prisoner of his father's enemy. One day, after many years, he was rescued and returned to his native land. All he knew up until then was the inside of a prison. He thought like a prisoner, he acted like a man under lock and key, and he was used to being given just enough to eek out a miserable existence. However, when he arrived at his ancestral home, he was shocked to be ushered into a magnificent palace, fed abundantly, and lavished with gifts. He didn't understand the freedom and blessings, and he became immediately uncomfortable and overwhelmed with royal life.

He shied away from any situation where he was expected to act like a king because he didn't feel like one. He still felt like a prisoner. He even longed for the confines of a prison because that was a world he understood. He knew his role as a captive without having to think about it. So, in some ways, the prison life was easier. However, day after day the constant encouragement from his servants and his father made him wonder if he really was who they said he was. One day, he looked in the mirror, dressed in his royal robes and thought to himself, "Today, I actually feel like a king." He went into the palace and, starting slowly, began to go about the business of ruling. He made a few decrees. He settled a few disputes, and over time he became comfortable in his new life. There was always the temptation to think it was all too good to be true or that it would be taken from him without warning; and some days he still fell back into the habitual fears of a prisoner. After years had passed, though, those moments became the exception rather than the rule, and he spent the rest of his days at his father's side, ruling over his kingdom.

Does that story ring a bell? It's you. You are the king (or queen) who was taken captive by an enemy and rescued by your Father. You are the one learning who you really are, so that you can rule and be confident in your identity. I'm sure the captive king in the story needed a little re-education — and so do we. So if you feel like you're in elementary school when you start your journey in the Spirit, please know that it's normal. Every week there are lessons for me to learn — and most of the time they stretch me to the "brain explosion" moment. Sometimes the Lord teaches me and sometimes His servants, the angels, are doing the instructing. But at all times they keep urging me to look in the mirror and see who I really am. I'm the king in the Garden. And they want me to feel like it.

CHAPTER 5

A WELL OF GRACE

If I have an arch-nemesis, it's that little voice in my head that tells me I've earned the good things in my life because of my outstanding behavior in some way. It's a very subtle delusion, and I think all of us have, at some point, believed that God was rewarding us based on our performance. If you catch us on the right day, sometimes we feel like our performance is pretty good. Then, when we feel like we've got our behaviors all worked out, we think, "If you get an "A" on your God report card, God will give you good things." I can always tell how much I'm buying into that false understanding when I screw up. When my behavior takes a turn and I start acting like a jackass, I suddenly get insecure in my relationship with the Lord. I think that all the blessings I have earned (prior to the behavioral screw-up) are suddenly in jeopardy. If you get an "F" on your God report card, shouldn't He do the "right" thing and take away your privileges?

Have you ever felt that way? It's a scary place to be, and after a big moral flop of one kind or another, I have spent many an hour trying to convince myself that He still loves me and I'm okay. As I mentioned before, when I started taking these journeys to the heavens, I felt like it was the best thing that ever happened to me; and, honestly, I felt a little privileged. I knew it was an unusual experience, so I felt an obligation to live up to it. To put it another way, I thought I had a responsibility to behave in a manner worthy of the calling. Would you like to guess how long it took me to fall short of my high standards? Even though I was experiencing heaven, I was not immune to the distractions of my flesh or the pride of my heart any more than before. So when those screw-up moments came along, I would go into a state of panic that I had just sinned my way right out of the greatest blessing of my life. Here is one example that plays out this pattern well.

One day, right before I left for the office, my wife and I got into an epic fight. In Christian terms, we call that a "marital discussion." I'm obliged to say that in this case, it was my fault. So I drove to my office with unresolved feelings of guilt and anger; and when I arrived, I knew the first thing I needed to do was pray. Prior to the "discussion," my plan was to have some time with my Lord in the Spirit and then get to the business of writing. Well, I didn't feel in the mood for a journey into the heavenlies, and it wasn't because I didn't want to go. I felt guilty and unworthy. The trips to the Garden, the palaces, and the walks with the Lord were all holy, special times. In that moment, I felt that if I tried to go up there, an angel would karate kick me back down in a hurry on account of my bad behavior. I paced around the office for about a half an hour before peeking open the eyes of my heart to see what Jesus was doing. Surprisingly, I saw his smiling face and his hands motioning me upward. He said, "Come up here with Me!"

I looked up to heaven and replied, "Did you just see what happened down here? How am I supposed to come up there when I just acted the way I did?" He didn't even acknowledge it. He just kept smiling and beckoning me upward. I fought His invitation for another thirty minutes or so until I said, "How does my foolishness not make You mad? How does it not cause some separation between us?" Jesus replied, "Just come up here and we'll talk about it." So I did. I sat down, closed my eyes, and was in the Spirit with my Lord. He sat there with me, smiling the way He does and treating me as if I was the most perfect thing He had ever seen. Then I asked Him that question again. "How does my foolishness not make You mad? How does it not cause at least some separation between us?"

He was sitting on my left; and in this moment I felt like a little kid compared to His tall, robust stature. He put His hand, palm up, in my lap, and I began to run my hands along the nail hole in the center of His palm. His hand was so big compared to mine, and it took both hands to feel His fingers, the knuckles, the flat of His palm, and down into the holes He still carried from His victory over the cross. Then He said, "Christopher, I didn't get off the cross early. I stayed on it until the work was done. I didn't cover 99% of the world's sins, but left just a little bit for you to pay penance for. I stayed until I had covered all sin for all people." I looked at His smiling face and said, "Lord, I know that You love me so much, and I know that You covered all my sin, but I still have the same question. How does my foolishness not make You mad? How does it not cause some separation between us?" I understood that He covered my sin, but I was still struggling with how He could be so happy with me when I felt like a total loser. So I didn't ask the question again because I didn't believe Him, I just didn't know how He could overlook my continuing misbehavior.

He turned to face me as we sat together and His expression changed. His smile was still there, but instead of communicating happiness, it started to convey a pleading kind of love.

43

In that pleading, direct tone, He said, "Christopher, God did get mad at your foolishness, and He took all of His anger out on Me at the cross so that He would never have to be mad at you again."

That answered my question and I held His nail-scarred hands with a new understanding. Jesus wasn't overlooking my ridiculous behavior. He didn't have to turn His head and pretend I didn't act the way I did towards my wife. All of the anger that would have been expressed at those shortcomings had been released on Him at the cross. There was no anger left for me. There was no Divine frown reserved for me on my bad days. It had all been poured out on my King, Jesus, at the cross — so that I could forever behold His smile. What a treasure! The God of all creation has stored up an eternity of smiles for me that I can never exhaust, no matter how foolish I act on earth. Now, one could argue that I could have received that same message simply by reading the scriptures. And that would be true. The message of Christ's total victory at the cross and our reconciliation to God is well described in the Bible. However, there is a difference between knowing something intellectually and knowing it deep down in your soul. Or, as I've heard it said, "A man with an experience is never at the mercy of a man with a theory." That day, Jesus' grace for me was no longer a theory.

As I mentioned before, walking around the Garden with the Father seemed like a heavy privilege to me; and I didn't want Him to think I was unworthy of the blessing. So I would try to live up to a moral standard (which I imposed upon myself) in the hopes of not loosing this rich blessing. This is a pretty common human condition. Many of us think that God likes us when we are doing good, and He is disappointed with us when we are bad. Or, in the case I've been describing above, that He would grant me access into the heavens when I was doing good, but keep me out when I'm misbehaving. If you're like me, it might take a few of these encounters to convince us of something other than our "eye for an eye" mentality. It just makes so much sense to our legalistic souls that God would reward us with blessings because we earned them — and that is exactly how the whole world system works. You get what you deserve. In short, God works differently.

I remember thinking about the phenomenon of grace one day while sitting in a coffee shop, when the Lord decided to interrupt my thoughts. I was pondering my journeys in the heavens in light of my spiritual failures on earth, when the Lord said to me, "Christopher, what did you do to earn the right to go up into the heavens in the Spirit?" I said, "I didn't do anything, Lord. You just started taking me up. I didn't ask for it or even know it was possible." Then He asked, "So, if you didn't do anything to earn it, how could you do anything to un-earn it?" In other words, since the blessing was not given because of my good behavior, how could it be taken away on account of my bad behavior?

There are some points in all of this that are particularly relevant as more and more people start to discover their literal access to heaven. First, as has been stated earlier, this is not just for the elite Christians who have it all together. If God can take you up to His throne room in the microseconds after you have done something horribly stupid — and He can — then this phenomenon has nothing to do with how good your behavior has been. You don't need a resume of holy living to earn a trip to the Garden. No amount of self-righteousness will do. We enjoy this access only through the incorruptible

Holy Spirit who has filled us. So in the most practical sense, start going to heaven as you are. Don't wait until you feel worthy (trust me, feeling deserving of it is just a mirage). Go as you are right now, with all your flaws. You will see, just like so many others, that Jesus is welcoming you with an enormous smile. Also, that goes for everyone else you know, particularly the ones that you think shouldn't be allowed into heaven at all!

Not too long ago, a friend of mine who was in Jerusalem met two girls traveling the world and looking for answers. They were not Christians, but they were looking for the truth in all the typical "New Age" ways. The wanted the real thing, so my friend ushered them into the spirit where they immediately had an encounter with Jesus. He revealed Himself to them with His huge smile and welcoming arms, despite their total rejection of Him up to that moment. The young lady starting weeping, realizing that Jesus was not waiting for her to be perfect, but He would take her as she was. So you see, God isn't making this harder than it needs to be!

Since this is such an important foundation, I'll give two more examples of times when God has really wanted me to get this. The first one came while I was in His throne room. I'll describe more of that environment later; but for now, I'll just tell you what He said that day. Jesus had brought me into the courts of the Father and up to His big throne. He walked me up the steps and the Father picked me up to sit with Him. That was a pretty big deal all by itself; and I didn't move a muscle while He held me in His grasp. Then, He pointed back down from the throne at Jesus and said, "His grace is not about acceptance through perfection, it's about acceptance through promise. This was another moment of learning that God's acceptance of us as His children, with rights to all of His bless-ings, is fully based on a promise, not on us becoming better hu-mans. Even though our relationship with Him will cause us to grow more and more like Him, his acceptance is not founded on that — lest we try to earn it or prove ourselves worthy of it.

The last example of this lesson came on a cool fall day. I was in the spirit walking around with Jesus when He took me back to the throne room. He ushered me to the Fa-ther and I was caught up in a whirlwind of His fiery presence. I felt surrounded by God — immersed in Him. It took the breath out of my body still sitting there on earth. Then, the strangest thing happened as His presence swirled around me: I suddenly wanted to leave. I didn't know why I started think-ing about all of the things I had to do, but I became preoccu-pied with ending the prayer time and getting on with my day.

Then I was instantly disappointed with myself. Here is God letting me into His glory and I suddenly wanted to leave! The whirlwind soon subsided and I found myself back in the Garden in a wonderful clearing surrounded by trees bearing hundreds of white flowers. Jesus walked up to me, and I immediately started apologizing about wanting to leave the throne room. I thought I had really messed up, but that's when Jesus smiled at me and said, "Son, this is where 'not good enough' becomes perfect because of the promise."

He put me at ease again. I had nothing to fear; but more importantly, I had nothing to prove. Since it's not about being "good enough," I could just relax and trust Him. It really was liberating to know that my behavior was not being graded. An A+ on your God report card won't get you a trip to heaven any more than an F will keep you out. Just trust Him and start going.

CHAPTER 6

THE KING'S BEDCHAMBER

There's something inspiring about walking into a magnificently large structure — and it's a different kind of inspiration than that of a natural wonder like the Grand Canyon or Niagara Falls. When you step into a cavernous building, you're aware that it's been fashioned out of the raw materials of the earth and that it took time and skill to build it. St. Peter's basilica in Rome is a good example of what I'm talking about. The ceilings are so high and the décor so ornate, that you wonder how humans were capable of building such a masterpiece. I've even been in train stations that wowed me with their grand entrances and vast, open spaces. Well, nothing compares to the buildings in heaven. They're at a whole other level of design, scope, and beauty.

As I got more comfortable seeing the details of things in the heavenly realms, I became enthralled with the places I was visiting. I made sure to take in each environment as I discovered it and I tried to take mental photographs of everything. There was one place I visited that overwhelmed my senses no matter how slow I took it in. I came to call it "Kingdom Palace," because it felt like the Lord's version of Capitol Hill. There were massive, ornate golden doors at the entrance and I walked with Jesus into a main room so big it could have held entire city blocks. The columns supporting the ceiling reached up so high it would make you dizzy trying to grasp the scope of it. The room had a rectangular shape, and at the far end was the Father's throne. All around me the room was buzzing with activity. Many of the figures moving about were certainly angels, but the constant bustle of the place made it hard to focus on any one thing. As Jesus was walking me through the crowd, He directed me down a hallway away from the grand room and all the activity. We arrived at a set of blue and gold doors, just as massive and ornate as the ones at the entrance, and walked in to a much quieter environment. The room was smaller and richly decorated, but there were no angels hustling around doing their work. It was just me and Jesus and that made it a lot easier to take it all in.

It was a bedroom, and it was extravagant. Everything looked gilded with gold, from the furniture to the designs in the ceiling and even the floor. Everywhere I looked, I saw only the finest materials and over the bed was a canopy of rich blues, purples, and reds. It was the bedchamber of a King. Jesus had spent those moments silently watching me roam about the room in awe. He wore His usual smile, like He always does when He knows He's showing me something that makes my jaw drop. Then, He walked over to the bed and sat down on it and then invited me to do the same. That's when it hit me. This was a bedroom. I was in Jesus' bedroom.

Suddenly, I had a sense of Jesus being the Bridegroom, and I, as a believer, being the Bride (*Ephesians 5: 22 – 33*). And, yes, that made me uncomfortable. I'm a married man, and I like being masculine. I didn't want this "bridal" understanding of the Church to be taken too far. He gave me the "don't worry" look and invited me to sit on the bed next to Him. As I did, the colorful fabric canopy dropped down to completely enclose the bed. We sat there in total privacy. Then, with His usual grin, Jesus said, "Christopher, don't think of marriage in terms of gender, think in terms of covenant." That explanation certainly made me feel better. It wasn't an affront to my masculinity to sit on this bed with Him because He was making a greater point about what marriage means in the context of God and man. We know what marriage is between a man and a woman on earth, but it also applies to Jesus and His Bride — His Church. But it stretches our brains a little to think of marriage on those terms; unless we understand it as a very specific kind of relationship with unequaled privileges. So, what does it mean to be married to God (especially if you're a man)? These were my thoughts:

- In marriage you share everything.
- In marriage you know each other intimately.
- The marriage relationship is different than every other relationship in life. It's the only one that enjoys those privileges above.

Jesus looked at me over His brow and said, "Christopher, that's what I want with you. I want to share everything I have with you. I want us to know each other intimately and I want this relationship and its privileges to be special."

That kind of unity is hard enough to imagine (and achieve) with an earthly spouse; but it's exactly what the Lord wants between us with Him. He brought me up on that bed just to prove to me that our relationship was more favorable than I had imagined. For instance, He wanted me to know that all of the amazing things He was showing me were to be shared with me, as if I had equal ownership of them. My journeys weren't an occasion for the Lord to say, "See this great palace, Chris? Too bad you can't have one, too." Rather, all the visits to the palace and the Garden were an introduction into a home He had already given me the deed to.

Before, I felt like a guest in His house; but after our talk in His bedchamber, I started to feel a sense of co-ownership. It's a subtle difference that I like to describe this way: When I started experiencing life in the Spirit, I would always have the sense, in the back of my mind, that I was getting away with something — like a fish taken out of the water and given a supernatural grace to breath air for a few minutes. Over time, I started to feel like a fish that belonged in the air just as much as in the water, and that breathing air wasn't unnatural; I was born to do it. So, after years of breathing the heavenly air, and after that much needed talk in the bedchamber, I knew I wasn't breaking any rules by being there. The Father had given me the Kingdom — the whole Kingdom — and that meant all the realms of heaven as well as the earth.

Our "marriage" talk made me feel more confident, too. It gave me the courage to stand up a little straighter when we walked into the throne room, and I didn't freak out as much when an angel made an appearance and wanted to talk. It was the beginning of learning how to be where I was in the Spirit and not just perceive it. Instead of getting a glimpse into another reality, I was learning to live in that other realm, just like the fish that could breath both the air and the water. However, I had some questions about the differences between the heavens and the earth. And to find out the answers, we had to go back to the throne room.

CHAPTER 7

THE THRONE ROOMS

There are lots of throne rooms to talk about. Every one of them has a specific atmosphere and purpose, and it could easily take a lifetime to discover all of them. On one visit, the Lord handed me a golden book called The Courts of Heaven. It looked hundreds of pages thick and read like an encyclopedia. On every page was a picture of a specific room and a paragraph or two describing its attributes. Here's one I got a chance to see myself: It was an all-white room with windows that were over fifty feet tall. Hung around the windows were long, white curtains that seemed to puff out with a gentle breeze. In the center of the room, on top of a staircase that approached from all four sides, sat the Lord on His throne. It was a quiet and comfortable place — the kind that makes you want to sit down and relax for a while. In fact, that was the purpose of that throne room; it was a place of rest. In the last chapter, I began to describe a very different place I called "Kingdom Palace." The main room — the one so big it could hold city blocks — was not necessarily for rest and relaxation.

To describe this place adequately, I need words that I'm not sure exist in the English language. It's just too big and too grand to provide a worthy description, but I'll give it a try. Imagine a huge, rectangular room with columns supporting either side of a high, vaulted ceiling. The columns themselves were imposing because of their size, and the whole room looked to be made of glowing gold. Nothing was left untouched by the hand of a master craftsman. Everywhere I looked, I would see ornate carvings and reliefs in various colors. Lining either side of the main walkway that led to the throne were huge, marble sculptures of angels and people, all depicting different parts of the story of God and His creation. The walkway that led to the throne was like a rich, red carpet and the throne itself was set atop a flight of wide stairs. Sometimes angels were standing on either side of the Lord as He held court; and at other times, the Lord would be milling about the grand room and talking with whoever was there.

About two-thirds of the way into the room, large hallways branched off to the right and the left, forming the shape of a cross. There, at that central intersection, was a gigantic spinning image of Earth. It was a globe over 100 feet high, and it rotated slowly just like the Earth does in space. Also, the earth had a soft, golden glow to it and I could see little golden lights flying around the globe's surface. It was like watching a real-time display of the heavenly activity going on all around planet Earth. Coupled with the constant activity in the room, it all had the feel of a government building where God's work was being planned and carried out.

As cool as the place is to look at, what sticks with me are the things Jesus and I have talked about while walking around that room. On one occasion, I walked up to the spinning earth and had this urge to touch it. Maybe it was the classic "put your finger in the electrical socket to see what happens" moment we all had as kids; but I think I just wanted to see what it was made of. At first, my hand went right through it, as if it was just a projected image. Then Jesus walked up to it and put His hand on it. To Him it was solid, which prompted me to try again. Sure enough, my hand found a solid substance as well. We stood there with our hands on this glowing blue and green globe while I pondered a question.

I had long wondered what heaven was made of. To me, the earth seemed very physical, and heaven seemed very ethereal. I don't know if I've been taught this or if it's just instinctual, but I have always thought of the spiritual realm as being very glorious but sort of intangible. The earth realm, on the other hand, I knew to be solid and touchable. So, to put it in different words, if the earth realm was made up of touchable, solid matter, then what was the spiritual, heavenly realm made of? Or I could say it this way: "If the earth is the material realm, are the heavens immaterial?"

In the tradition of His people, Jesus answered my questions with a question of His own. He said, "Christopher, where is My physical body right now?" I answered, "Aha! Your actual, physical body is up here in the heavenly realms, seated at the right hand of God." Affirming, Jesus said, "Right. My physical, resurrected body, with all its bones and material substance, is existing in the highest heavens, where we are talking right now."

So the heavenly realms I had come to discover were not some intangible place made of spiritual energy where apparitions floated about. Rather, it had the same touchable substance of the earth realm. Think about it this way. If Jesus' flesh and bones are seated on a throne in the heavenly places (*Hebrews 12: 2*), then the throne He is sitting on must have the same physical and material properties that He has. One was not the "physical" realm and the other the "spiritual" realm. They were both physical. They were both touchable. An actual physical body, just like the resurrected version that Jesus took with Him when He ascended (and it was certainly physical... see *John 20: 26-29*) could exist very comfortably in the highest heavens. That means the trees in the Garden, the columns in the throne room, and the throne itself are not spiritual projections, they were made of substance in the same way things are on the Earth. All this is to say that, whatever differences there are between the heavens and the earth, it is not a case of one realm being more solid than the other. There is solid stuff in both.

Now I had to ask another question. "If the heavens are just as material and touchable as the Earth, what makes them different than the earthly realm?" With a really sly grin, Jesus said, "Height." I couldn't get Him to clarify what He meant; but I could tell (mostly by the grin) that it was a play on words. He was not talking about "height" in terms of elevation or altitude, but of something else entirely. I guessed that He was speaking in dimensional terminology for a reason — even if he didn't mean a spatial dimension in the way we would think of it. You can ponder this on your own if you like, but the heavenly realms are likely in different dimensions, best described from God's perspective as varying levels or "heights" of dimensions. Brain explosion anyone?

All of this had a more practical implication too, which came up after that talk in the throne room. It started with Jesus saying to me, "Stop looking for your answers down there on earth. All the answers are up here." He continued, "Look at my life when I was on the earth. I was always looking up here for my guidance." If you will recall, some of the first lines in this book were about how hard it is to stop looking at all the earthly things vying for our attention — and I'm sure Jesus sensed my reluctance to let go of an earth-centered perspective. We spend every moment on Earth touching and sensing things, so thinking of the heavenly realm as being as substantial, as important, and even as "real" as the earth realm is quite a challenge. I certainly thought so. Even though I was rapidly discovering the heavenly realms, it was hard to think of them as more than an accessory to earthly life. Almost like it was the icing on the cake — but the cake was still on the earth.

To help me understand, He put it another way. "Christopher, if one realm is going to seem more real to you, shouldn't it be the one that I and the Father are sitting enthroned in right now as we speak?" He had a good point. If one of these dimensions should be considered the most "real," wouldn't it be the one that Jesus Himself is currently resting in? If one realm is going to be considered more substantial, wouldn't it be the one that contains a throne of such substance that it can hold up the presence of the Almighty?

Heaven is My throne and the earth is My footstool. (Isaiah 66:1)

When I pondered that, I realized that no matter how much I am tempted to define my existence by what's happening on the Earth, I should be more aware, more in tune, and more consciously present in the realm made of greater substance. To put it in scriptural terms, read this passage again from *2 Corinthians*:

For momentary, light affliction is producing for us an eternal weight of glory far beyond all comparison, while we look not at

the things which are seen, but at the things which are not seen;
for the things which are seen are temporal, but the things which
are not seen are eternal. (2 Corinthians 4: 17-18)

The temporal, fading things are in the "seen" earthly realm. The eternal, lasting, substantial things are in the "unseen" heavenly realms. Which one do you want to live in?

Now, if you're wondering how all this fits together, let me make this point: When we are up there in the Spirit, we are not up there in our bodies. Remember the cases of John, Elisha, Isaiah, and Ezekiel. Their bodies were on earth while they perceived something heavenly. The big shift comes in realizing that the things you perceive in the Spirit are more solid and substantial than the things you perceive in your body. For now, your biological body can't see or interact with heaven — it just senses the things on Earth. However, the Holy Spirit inside of you has no such limitations. I'm not saying that this is an easy shift to make, either. We have spent so much time living our lives in our fading, earthly bodies and perceiving nothing else, that when we start looking in the Spirit, we categorize it as a "visionary experience" and not an actual visit to an actual place. So let me assure you of this wonderful fact: You might be making the trip only in your spirit — but you are actually making the trip. And the place that you are visiting is not only real, it's more solid than the earth under your feet.

Heaven isn't just a realm to be glimpsed while we feel anchored here on earth. It's time to let the anchor loose and find our dwelling place in the heavens — where the homes, palaces, and throne rooms are every bit as real and substantial as those found on the Earth.

CHAPTER 8

CHOIR PRACTICE

I like it when the Lord explains things to me — and I don't think He ever has to worry about me running out of questions. Not that He minds me asking. He even encourages it. Remember, He wants to share all of this with us, so giving Him the space to be our teacher is a role He relishes. He's really good at it, too, and He uses all kinds of methods to get His point across. For instance, did you know that most people don't learn all that well being lectured, but are able to retain and apply tons of information if there's an activity to reinforce the point? It's that classic principal again: "A man with an experience is not at the mercy of a man with a theory." Well, the point the Lord wanted me to get was this: Heaven is a real place that I was really visiting. The activity that came with that lesson had to do with how one realm affects the other. In our journeys together, I started to see things in the heavenly places come down to the Earth and immediately have an effect of my life there.

One instance occurred while I was writing *Caught Up in the Spirit*. Since I was getting more comfortable being in the heavens, I would start my day with a heavenly journey; and Jesus was always gracious enough to end it in a place that seemed just perfect for writing. So He would invite me to stay there all day as I worked, even while my body was sitting in front of a computer screen. While I was typing away, I would occasionally close my eyes and see a quiet part of the Garden or an ornate study or wherever He had led me to that day. It made work so pleasant, sitting there with Him and talking together as I wrote. After I finished a section, I would send it off to the editor to be tweaked and wait for His response. There was one section in particular in the book that was very pesky. It was about four pages long and full of material that was a little hard to explain. Consequently, it kept getting sent back to me with a request to make it all clearer, and I honestly didn't know how to do that. Fortunately, Jesus did.

After about four re-writes it still wasn't right, and I arrived at the office one morning planning to give it another try. However, before I even got started, an angel appeared in the room to greet me. He was dressed in white and gold, and as far as I could see, he looked like a man. He invited me up to the heavens with him and so I went. We had a short walk through the Garden, and I mostly just followed him in silence. I wasn't quite sure what the protocol was when being led around the heavenly places by an angel. Are we allowed to talk? Does Jesus have to be here for me to trust you're a good angel? I think those are pretty normal questions to have.

Eventually, we arrived at a palatial building, and although it was big and glorious, it looked different than the Kingdom Palace I had come to know. We walked through the doors, which were made of dark, thick wood, and into a cathedral-like environment. You could have heard a pin drop in this peaceful place. It wasn't super bright inside either, just a warm glow, and on either side of a central aisle leading to the front were rows and rows of pews. "Pews?" I asked. I don't know what I expected to see up there that day, but a cathedral full of pews was not it. I can remember many a boring Sunday morning sitting in a church pew, so that had a negative connotation in my mind. I was in for a shock, though.

The angel led me down the central aisle about halfway to the front, and then we both worked our ways to the middle of one of the long pews and sat down. At that moment, we seemed to be the only ones there. Then I noticed that at the very front of the room were massive, gold organ pipes, and there were layers of them stacked in ascending and descending order. I looked at the angel sitting on my right and said, "What is this place and what are we doing here?" All I got in return was a sly, knowing grin. It's that same smile Jesus gives me when He knows something I don't, and isn't exactly in the mood to reveal all the mysteries just yet. So we waited there and then... Boom!

Suddenly the organ lets out an enormous blast of sound and a heavenly choir, which I had not previously seen sitting to the right and left of the organ pipes, erupted with those famous lines from Handel's "Messiah":

King of kings! Forever and ever! And Lord of lords!
Hallelujah! Hallelujah!

The sheer volume was enough to scare me silly, and the angel, now laughing slightly, looked at me and said, "Choir practice." He then went on to explain, "This choir of angels is practicing for Jesus' return. They will sing this for Him when goes back to Earth."

So as I sat and listened to heavenly choir practice (all of which was Handel's "Messiah" by the way), I noticed Jesus entering the front of the room. He stood there by the first row of pews and talked with another angel dressed in white. Then

He seemed to notice me sitting halfway back and motioned for me to come up and talk with Him. Jesus sat down with me on that front pew and opened a black folder. Inside was the four-page section of my book that I didn't know how to fix. On every page, Jesus had taken a red pen and corrected things. He had scratched out some words and added in other phrases and paragraphs. As we sat there, He took the time to go over the section with me page by page. When we were done I couldn't wait to open my earthly eyes again and get right to work. I think I yelled goodbye to Him as I bolted passed all the pews and out the door. Back in my office, I immediately fired up the computer, made the corrections, and sent it in. Within a few days, I got an email from the editor saying the section was perfect.

A few things started to come together in all of this. First, I was able to clearly read what Jesus wrote on His copy of my manuscript, just like the scriptures and other books He gave me in the Garden. The heavenly school was paying off in a big way. Second, this qualified as proof. It was an example of something from the heavens directly affecting my earthly environment. I didn't have to wait long before something else happened along those same lines. I'm going to share a few more of these crossover events, and I'm sure you'll see the same trend that I did — all of these testimonies involve angels.

CHAPTER 9

MESSENGERS FROM HEAVEN

It's a fairly common experience for kids to have some emotional difficulty when another child is brought into the family. When our son was born, our two-year old daughter had a bit of a problem adjusting to the shift. She was used to having all of mom and dad's focus, and now there was a very needy infant competing for our time (and winning in most cases). Two-year old children don't have many tricks up their sleeve, but the one they know well is the classic temper tantrum. My daughter employed this to great effect, and in those first couple of months after our son came into the world, life was very interesting around the house. We had tried almost everything to correct the bad behavior and reassure her of her importance in the family, but we were out of ideas. What we found out is that our daughter needed help from heaven. Specifically, she needed help from an angel. Here is how it happened.

It was a normal day in the Garden with the Lord. We were walking along a covered pathway lined with columns. I was watching the birds and butterflies fly all around us. The birds were a bright blue and the butterflies a striking violet. As we walked together, I asked the Lord if He was taking me somewhere. He told me that all He wanted to do was walk and talk with me. There wasn't an agenda or place we had to be; and the connection between us was so comfortable that we just walked along and talked like any two friends would. Somewhere in the conversation it occurred to me that it was a good time to make some requests; and since my daughter was ever present on my mind, I thought to ask about her first.

Without knowing it, I went into "prayer mode." I stopped talking to Him as a friend and started treating Him as if He were some distant deity that I had to be formal with in order to get what I wanted. Instead of the easy, comfortable speech, I started using phrases like, "Lord, I just pray for my daughter that she would get better…" Immediately, the Lord stopped walking, looked directly at me and said, "Don't say 'pray,' just talk to me." So, I turned to Him and said as bluntly as I would with any one of my best friends, "I need help with my daughter, and I have no idea what I'm doing here." As soon as the words left my mouth I watched an angel fly to Jesus' side. He whispered something to the angel, who then immediately flew off again. It all happened in a flash, and I had to ask the Lord what just transpired. Jesus didn't answer me in audible words, but in my head He communicated this scripture:

> See that you do not despise one of these little ones, for I say to you that their angels in heaven continually see the face of My Father who is in heaven. (Matthew 18:10)

The angel who flew to Jesus' side was my daughter's angel. She was a "little one" with an angel who always saw the face of the Father; and now Jesus had sent that angel off with whispered instructions. I wondered if and when I would see any impact from that experience; but within a few hours, my wife called me at my office and said, "I don't know what's happened! Our daughter is completely different!" Our daughter's behavior had changed; and as time went on, we never had to revisit those issues with her again. I never did find out what instructions were given to that heavenly messenger; but because the result was so immediate and lasting, I never gave it much thought. I did think about this though — if my children had angels assigned to them, and all it takes is a talk with the Lord in the Garden for those messengers to be empowered and instructed, why not take full advantage of that when there is a need? That's a great thought, but I had to learn to be confident in these interactions, and it took a few more encounters for that to happen. Here is another crossover event that helped me realize the importance of co-laboring angels:

I had a friend in another city and she was sick. She had pain in her sides and her back and the doctors didn't have any answers, even after a barrage of tests. One morning, she had left a message for me asking for prayer; I figured I would bring it up during that day's trip to heaven. Just before noon, I took a break from work and went up to a heavenly city. All the structures were pure white and situated around a high hill. Jesus walked me up through the streets to the very top of the city, where we entered a palatial building. We walked into a large room with an ornate marble floor, and engraved into the marble was a compass pointing to the four cardinal directions. The room itself was circular, and about half of it opened up to the outside so you could look over the white city. Through that semi-circular opening angel after angel flew in until they all but filled the whole room.

The angels were all different shapes and sizes. Some had wings, others didn't, and some even had colorful jewels placed on their chest or on their foreheads. It was a beautiful gathering and for a while I just walked among them, taking mental notes of what I saw. In the back of the room, away from the opening to the outside, Jesus sat down on a throne. He invited me to sit next to Him, and when I did, the angels started approaching the throne. The first one was dressed in white, with a shinning red ruby in the center of his breast. He stretched out his wings and waited there, I presumed for a word from Jesus. That's when it got interesting. There are so many moments in the heavens when I feel like everyone knows something but me. Sometimes it's comical, and I never mind because it is always a moment where I find out something else about my Lord that blesses me. In this case, the thing everyone knew but me, is that the angels were waiting on me to say something.

Jesus walked me to where the angel was standing before the throne, and then told me to put my hand on the angel's chest and bless him. I felt totally unqualified for this job but I did it anyway. As I blessed him, he seemed to radiate even brighter, and if those wings could stretch out any farther, they did in that moment. He looked energized, and when I was done, he flew out of the circular assembly room and into the sky. For a few minutes Jesus and I met every angel that came up to the throne and blessed them as well. Some were given instructions too, even though I didn't know what I was going to say until they were standing there in front of me.

One by one, the angels flew out after they received a blessing; and when the room was empty again, Jesus and I left as well. We walked back down through the city and came to a bridge overlooking an infinitely deep chasm. I instinctually knew that the bridge led back to the earth realm, and the chasm was the gap between the dimensions. In that moment, I became sad. I didn't want to leave Jesus' presence or that wonderful city. It was the first time I can remember thinking that I wanted to be there more than here. Jesus heard my unspoken request and took me to a little courtyard close to the bridge and the chasm. That's when it dawned on me — I should talk to the Lord about my sick friend before I leave this place!

Having learned the lesson about needless formality, I just started telling Jesus about the voice mail my friend had left me that morning. All I did was recite the symptoms she told me she was experiencing; and while I was talking, Jesus pulled out a little pad and pen and began writing. When I finished, he pulled out the page like a doctor would with a prescription pad and handed it to an angel who had just joined our meeting. The angel took the note and flew across the chasm to the earth realm. After a short talk with Jesus, I also took the bridge back over the chasm and opened my earthly eyes and went back to work. About twenty minutes later, I got a text message from my friend saying she felt 100% better and wanted to know if I had been praying for her. I wasted no time calling her up to tell her about the angel flying over with Jesus' prescription, which prompted her to wonder what He had written on that note. I told her to ask for herself, and she did the next morning. The Lord showed her the small piece of paper. And written on it were the words:

RELEASE HER.

I smiled while I imagined the interaction between the

angel and whatever dark presence had been causing my friend all that pain. She was being hounded by some devil; and all that was needed was for a heavenly messenger to show up with specific instructions from the King. When the angel handed that evil spirit the note, he had no choice but to let her go and stop bothering her. Maybe something similar happened with my daughter. In both cases, a ministering spirit flew across the divide between realms and brought an immediate and lasting blessing. My daughter stopped throwing tantrums; and my friend never had that pain again. As for me, I learned about interacting with the angels, and this experience was my first time seeing them assemble together before going about their work. It was a scene I would grow very familiar with as I got to know these spirit beings and how they co-labor with us.

Since it's always helpful to gain some scriptural context, let's look at a few passages that describe Jesus' familiarity with the ministering spirits:

> *While I was still speaking in prayer, then the man Gabriel, whom I had seen in the vision previously, came to me in my extreme weariness about the time of the evening offering. He gave me instruction and talked with me and said, "O Daniel, I have now come forth to give you insight with understanding. (Daniel 9: 21 – 22)*

> *Then Jesus said to him, "Go, Satan! For it is written, 'You shall worship the Lord your God, and serve Him only.'" Then the devil left Him; and behold, angels came and began to minister to Him. (Matthew 4: 10 – 11)*

Then Jesus said to him, "Go, Satan! For it is written, 'You shall worship the Lord your God, and serve Him only.'" Then the devil left Him; and behold, angels came and began to minister to Him. (Matthew 4: 10 – 11)

"...You will see greater things than these." And He said to him, "Truly, truly, I say to you, you will see the heavens opened and the angels of God ascending and descending on the Son of Man." (John 1: 50 – 51)

Then Jesus said to him, "...Or do you think that I cannot appeal to My Father, and He will at once put at My disposal more than twelve legions of angels? (Matthew 26: 51-53)

I think it's easy for Christians to conceptualize that there are thousands of angels in heaven; and at God's (or Jesus') discretion, they help us out on earth as well. Maybe it was the time a stranger came out of nowhere to help us, or perhaps that time we just barely missed being in a car accident... Most of us believers have stories of an incident of where we think an angel might have been involved. But what if the interaction between us and them is more personal than that? What if certain spirits are specifically assigned to us for our whole sojourn here on planet earth? What if they know us as well as our best friends, having watched us and served us for years? And what if they can be appreciated as individual living creatures, too, with proper names and different personalities? In the next chapters, we will talk about discovering a friendship with angels. I was shocked to find out this was even possible, but I was pleased to learn that there were plenty of believers before me who had enjoyed this very thing.

CHAPTER 10

KNOWING ANGELS

There was a very big change about 2,500 years ago. Historically speaking, the nation of Israel had been besieged by the Babylonian empire and finally defeated. As a result, many people were taken captive back to Babylon — and among them was a young man named Daniel. He and his friends stayed true to the Lord despite their hardships, and their experiences make up some of the first stories many of us heard in Sunday school. There are the classics like Daniel in the Lion's den, and Shadrach, Meshach, and Abednego being delivered from the fiery furnace; but there was another story brewing during these times, and it had to do with angels. We only have to wait until about halfway through the book of Daniel before the big change starts to happen. The first instance occurs below, right after the prophet Daniel had a vision of the future.

> *When I, Daniel, had seen the vision, I sought to understand it;*
> *and behold, standing before me was one who looked like a man.*
> *And I heard the voice of a man between the banks of Ulai,*
> *and he called out and said, "Gabriel, give this man an understanding of the vision." (Daniel 8: 15 – 16)*

I know most of us already have some thoughts on who Gabriel is, but just put yourself in Daniel's shoes for a minute. He was used to seeing visions and having dreams in his role as a prophet. However, this was the first time he had some extra help interpreting what he saw — and it wasn't the last. It happens again in the very next chapter:

> *While I was still speaking in prayer, then the man Gabriel, whom I had seen in the vision previously, came to me in my extreme weariness about the time of the evening offering. He gave me instruction and talked with me and said, "O Daniel, I have now come forth to give you insight with understanding. (Daniel 9: 21 – 22)*

It must have been cool to see the same angel twice; but in the next chapter, Daniel learns about other spirits acting on his behalf. In that passage, it isn't just about Daniel understanding a vision from God, it's about a whole battle being waged in the atmosphere above him.

> *I lifted my eyes and looked, and behold, there was a certain man dressed in linen, whose waist was girded with a belt of pure gold of Uphaz. His body also was like beryl, his face had the appearance of lightning, his eyes were like flaming torches, his arms and feet like the gleam of polished bronze, and the sound of his words like the sound of a tumult... Then he said to me, "Do not be afraid, Daniel, for from the first day that you set your heart on understanding this and on humbling yourself before your God, your words were heard, and I have come in response to your words. But the prince of the kingdom of Persia was withstanding me for twenty-one days; then behold, Michael, one of the chief princes, came to help me, (Daniel 10:*

5-13)

This report on what was happening in the heavenly realms is a big deal, but it's still not the change I mentioned earlier. Remember, Isaiah and Ezekiel saw angels, too. Here is the big shift. From the beginning of Genesis to the time of Daniel, there are twenty-seven books of the Bible spanning about 3,500 years of history; yet this is the first time — ever — that angels are known by their proper name.

Prior to the scriptures just mentioned, none of the Biblical stories involving angels distinguish one spirit from another. Simply calling this spirit messenger "Gabriel" or "Michael" meant that he was a specific person with a specific personality. He was an entity to be known, not just categorized as some vague force of nature. I would be so bold as to call this the single greatest leap in man's understanding of the angelic realm — simply because it starts an actual relationship. Giving someone your name is the first crucial step in an introduction, and you can choose to offer it or stay anonymous. With Daniel, the angels chose to be known.

It shouldn't be lost on us, either, that Daniel's encounters with these messengers occurred in the spiritual realm. Go back and read the book of *Daniel* for yourself. All of his encounters are described as visions. On one occasion, he makes sure to tell us that none of his companions saw what he did. That's because these things weren't seen with earthly, biological eyes. Daniel was seeing with those internal, spiritual eyes we've talked so much about. Yet, all of these encounters were as real as anything else the prophet would have known; and that comes across clearly in the writing. Getting back on topic though, let's look at the effect of this shift in the years following Daniel's ministry.

Again, keep in mind there were no recorded names for angels for 3,500 years of Bible history. Daniel opened the door with the first two — Gabriel and Michael — and in the years following, the list grew exponentially. Raphael and Uriel were two names given in various apocryphal writings. Then the Book of Enoch surfaced. Although it's a little known book, it was widely read and respected all the way up to Jesus' day and after. Bible scholars readily admit that there are concepts in the New Testament that owe their origin to this book, which began circulation just after Daniel's period of history. In the book of *Enoch*, we have the four angels previously mentioned, only now Enoch clues us in that these are the four archangels situated around the throne. Enoch also mentions others by name, even some of the angels that fell. Amazingly, the whole book can be considered one long conversation with a few different angels, notably, Uriel the archangel.

And, it doesn't stop there. In the gospels, Luke reports that it was Gabriel who told Mary she was chosen to be the mother of Jesus. Finally, in Revelation, John sees lots of different angels, and he mentions Michael by name when he describes a war in heaven. If we are just going by shear numbers, then John wins the prize for most angelic interaction in one setting. Fitting, isn't it, that the last canonized book of the Bible is more angel-oriented than any before it?

Even though Daniel was a prisoner in Babylon, he ended up leaving his angelic knowledge with that culture, too. After his death, the Babylonians and Persians began associating the four archangels with the four "royal stars" found in well-known constellations. Also, it has been put forth that the wise men (or magi) who came from the east to find the infant Jesus got their astronomical information from Daniel's teachings, passed down through generations of Persian wise men. Could all of these historical changes be traced back to Daniel?

I think it's very likely, since he was the one who kickstarted this whole process. And there's one more thing I'd like to point out from Daniel's life before we move on. It involves Michael, and here are the two scriptures where it happens:

> *So he said, "Do you know why I have come to you? Soon I will return to fight against the prince of Persia, and when I go, the prince of Greece will come; but first I will tell you what is written in the Book of Truth. (No one supports me against them except Michael, your prince. (Daniel 10: 20-21)*

> *"At that time Michael, the great prince who protects your people, will arise. (Daniel 12:1)*

The word, "prince," is used to describe a type of angel. You could think of it like a rank in the angelic chain of command. In the first passage, we learn there are two angelic princes fighting each other: Michael and the prince of Persia. In the second passage, we hear of Michael being a "great prince." This is the forerunner of the term "archangel." Truthfully, I like the princely description better. It's a better term for the job Michael is doing since the word "angel" simply means "messenger." We'll get into that later. For now, just look at the relationship between Daniel and Michael. Michael is not just a random high prince of heaven — he's presented to Daniel as "your prince."

Try to put yourself in Daniel's shoes one more time.

It must have been very encouraging to know there was a high prince in heaven just for him and his people, and it tells us that the relationship between "us" and "them" can be very personal. "Your," is a possessive pronoun that implies specificity and exclusiveness. It makes us realize that angels aren't just flying about haphazardly to see who needs help. Rather, they are attached to us as individuals, or as families, or as a people. Knowing that they are there and that they are "yours" is a rich blessing.

CHAPTER 11

A PRINCE FOR ME

I have an interest in early Irish Christianity. Those who research it claim it might have been a bright spot in what history calls the "Dark Ages." That's such an ominous term for a period, but it does adequately describe some aspects of life after the fall of the Roman Empire (around 470 AD). The mainstream Christian church at this time had fallen very far from what it was at the beginning. It had become religious and full of legalistic traditions. However, Christianity in Ireland was different. Maybe it was the location, flung out in the Atlantic and far from the centers of civilization; but whatever the reason, it remained "un-romanized" and unusually vibrant during a time of regression elsewhere.

The reason I'm bringing it up here is because we can find a continuation of the things we've been talking about in the previous chapter. Angelic involvement didn't stop with Daniel, the book of *Enoch*, *Luke*, and John's *Revelation*. It carried on in a group of Irish Apostles perched on the edge of the known world. St Patrick, for instance, is as Irish as it gets; and his story is worth researching on your own. Early on in his journey, he meets an angel who gives him some instruction, and just like Daniel's experience, the angel gives his name. This heavenly spirit, called Victoricus, met with Patrick often. An old 6th century book called the

The Life of Patrick, calls Victoricus "his faithful old friend." That sounds pretty familiar and personal. Also, in that same book, we learn Patrick had a weekly meeting with an angel and "enjoyed speaking with him as one man speaks to another."

Another Irish apostle, St. Columba, had similar experiences. He founded the historic monastery on the island of Iona in the 6th century, and it was there that someone observed him having an angelic conference. This was the observer's report as recorded in the *Life of Columba*.

> For Holy angels, citizens of the celestial country, flying to him with wonderful swiftness, and clothed in white robes, began to stand around the holy man as he prayed; and after some conversation with the blessed man, that heavenly host, as if perceiving itself to be under observation, quickly sped back to the highest heavens.

Patrick and Columba are great post-biblical examples of someone having a personal interaction with a heavenly spirit. It even feels like the quality of relationship between man and angel is still progressing, even in those Dark Ages. Speaking of angels as "old faithful friends" is one more leap forward in closeness and connection.

I found these Irish testimonies to be very beneficial because it helped me understand what was happening to me as I journeyed in the Spirit. As I mentioned before, I had seen angels go from heaven to earth to heal my friend or help my daughter. But one day I ventured up to heaven and met an angel I would eventually call a friend. On this particular day, Jesus and I were walking across a translucent gold bridge on our way to the heavenly city. It would not surprise me at all if it was the same New Jerusalem that John describes in *Revelation*. The whole city was illuminated with a golden color, and even though I had seen it before, the beauty of it still stunned me. We walked up to one of the gates of the city, and right before we entered, Jesus turned around and stopped. There, standing to my left, was an angel. He was dressed in a deep purple robe, and he wore a silvery crown with an amethyst jewel set in the center. The angel kneeled down before Jesus, and to my total surprise, Jesus took the crown off and put it on my head. If you're shocked like I was hang on — because all of this has a really good explanation.

I had never had an angel give me any gift, much less a crown, and it did feel very personal — kind of like wearing someone else's clothes. I asked Jesus if I could know his name, and Jesus prompted him to tell me. He called himself Breanadan; and in the ensuing months he became a regular presence in the spiritual journeys. He walked with Jesus and I around the Garden, he journeyed with us to the palaces, and on occasion, Jesus would send the two of us off by ourselves. In all honesty, I had to be coaxed into this. It took constant affirmation from Jesus that I was still on the right path. Historical references aside, this was a totally different experience for me. Over time, it became comfortable and enjoyable, and it was the beginning of a lasting friendship.

I learned that Breanadan was a wonderful navigator and he took on the job of showing me around heaven. With every journey I began to feel more at home up there, which goes right back to what we have talked about in previous chapters. So much of life in the Spirit is about learning who you are and where you belong. The Apostle Paul called us "citizens of heaven" (*Philip-*

pians 3:20), so it was pretty clear where he thought our home was.

Traveling with my angelic friend revealed more of my heavenly home than I had previously seen, almost like the grace to navigate the heavenly places came by wearing his crown. That, in turn, is what made me feel like an actual citizen of heaven. In other words, it's hard to feel like a card-carrying heavenly citizen when you don't know what that place is like. Would you feel like a true citizen of your own country on earth if you had never seen it or spent any significant time there? Would you feel like an American if you had never been to America?

Additionally, it was the discovery of my true home that also revealed my true self. It's a wonderful thing to see yourself as you really are, not as the fading biological shell that covers us on this earth; and the more I journeyed with Breanadan, the more I started to feel and even look like a heavenly citizen. When I would see myself in the Spirit, I appeared bright and eternal. I even started to notice a crown on my head that looked a little different than the one Breanadan gave me. One day, the Lord took Breanadan's crown off for good — and I felt like a kid whose dad just took the training wheels off of his bicycle. When I asked the Lord why it was necessary to wear Breanadan's crown for a time, He said, "Christopher, you had to wear Breanadan's crown in order to see your own."

Breanadan had a few things to say about Jesus as well. One day we were all sitting together and I just couldn't stop staring at Jesus. He was radiant, and it was one of those moments when you are just taken by the majesty of the King of kings and the Lord of lords. In that breathless moment, I turned to Breanadan and asked, "What do I have to do to get closer to Jesus, because He is just amazing!"

Breanadan smiled at me and said, "Christopher, Jesus is like gravity. There is nothing you need to do to get closer to Him. Once you are in His pull, once you are in His orbit, He just draws you in with His love and power." My angel friend then went on to say, "Everyone on the earth is being drawn to Him, whether they know it or not. Everyone is on a collision course with Jesus. For some, it will be a violent end, like a meteor burning up in the atmosphere; but for others, it will be a graceful kiss when Jesus and mankind touch. Once you are in his orbit, Christopher, there is nothing you need to do. Just let Him keep drawing you in closer and closer." For a Physics student like myself, Breanadan could not have said it any more poetically than that. It was so simple. Jesus is like gravity. He draws everyone to Himself.

By the way, when I first met Breanadan I thought his name might mean something. Certainly the angels listed in the Bible have meaningful names. However, the name "Breanadan" is not of English origin, so I had to search a bit in some other languages to find it. Turns out, it's Irish — Gaelic — and it means "prince."

CHAPTER 12

HIGH PRINCES,
PRINCES, AND POWERS

Did you know there is a whole study of angels called "angelology?" It might be a more recent term, but it describes an age-old interest in the structure and rules of the angelic realm. It seems that every religion or sect that acknowledges the existence of spiritual beings has made an attempt to classify them with varying results. Maybe it's that innate desire to know and categorize the otherworldly things that leads us to form an official chain of command. This is just my opinion, but I think forming an "official" angelic hierarchy is like trying to do calculus after just learning the numbers one-through-ten. Is it possible to get it right? Yes, but it's not likely.

This is just my opinion as well, but I'm not sure the people responsible for the traditional angelic orders are the ones who actually visited the heavenly realms and talked with them. There's just something about those classic spiritual hierarchies that feels a bit institutional; and that's why I don't put much stock in them. For contrast's sake, *Daniel*, the book of *Enoch*, and John's *Revelation* were authored by people with first-hand experience. And none of them give us an "official" order.

Don't hold your breath because I'm not going to give it a shot, either. I'm not saying it shouldn't be investigated, I'm just not sure we have all the information yet to do it justice. It's my belief that in the days ahead, more and more people will discover their unhindered connection to heaven. Therefore, I'll wait until more of us have had conversations with angels before forming a working model of their relational structure. For now, I'll share with you what I've learned — and I believe it is far from complete. At the time of this writing, I've been introduced to dozens of ministering spirits of different levels of authority. There is certainly an order in how they have presented themselves; but again, I do not believe it is an exhaustive list.

There's one more thing I'd like to bring up before we get into all of that, and it's the issue of calling them "angels." There's nothing wrong with it because it gets used in the scriptures almost every time they show up. We get the word from the Greek term "angelos," and there is a Hebrew equivalent as well. In both languages, it just means "messenger." The only problem is that not all of them seem to have that job. The great theologian, St. Augustine, must have seen the same issue. In a commentary on the *Psalms* he wrote, "Angel is the name of an activity, while spirit denotes a nature." Also, the author of Hebrews makes a similar statement:

> *Are they not all ministering spirits, sent out to render service for the sake of those who will inherit salvation? (Hebrews 1:14)*

In my experience, it just feels right to think of them as spirits who have many different occupations. Certainly some of them are messengers; but there are lots of other activities these heavenly spirits can be observed doing as well.

For instance, Breanadan is a wonderful guide. If there was a heavenly G.P.S. system up there, he wouldn't need it, because he knows his way around perfectly. I learned from watching him that spirits don't fly around wherever they want to; but — just like us — they follow established roads. Think of it like driving your car. As much as we would like to take our family sedan off-roading, it wouldn't work very well after the first mile (if that). We have to keep it on the road to have an efficient journey. In the same way, they also travel on well-known pathways. To me, those pathways look like currents, so maybe a sailboat flowing in a prevailing wind is a better metaphor than a car on an asphalt road. Either way, it was Breanadan's job to know the roadmap; and it seems he had a hand in building and maintaining those pathways as well.

In our travels together he introduced me to other spirits, many of whom where either his peers or subordinates. If you will recall, Breanadan gave me his name in Gaelic, and it meant "prince." By the time a few months had passed, I had met two more princes and about nine other angels whom Breanadan called "powers." Again, I'm not trying to fit this into a hierarchy; but it does seem that the spirits known as princes carried more authority than the powers. If you're doing the math, that made three princes and nine powers for a total of twelve angels. That seemed significant to me, almost like I was meeting a full team of spirits; but in actuality, it felt more like a family unit. They had a relationship that went beyond heavenly co-workers. The princes acted like brothers and the powers seemed like their children.

There's always an elegant symmetry between heaven and earth. In this case, I noticed a correlation between this family of angels and Jesus and His apostles. During Jesus' ministry, He hand-picked twelve men to follow Him, and of those twelve, there were three who were extra close to Him. Whenever He needed to take a few of them aside and talk about something, it would be those three. They were the trusted inner-circle. When I saw the three angelic princes and the nine powers under them, I couldn't help but think I was seeing a heavenly order. The numbers "12" and "3" are very special to the Lord, and He uses them all the time to express different aspects of His government and character.

As I got to know this family of angels, I learned to distinguish them by their color. Breanadan was very purple. His robe, his hair, and the amethyst jewel in his crown all had the same hue. Others appeared dressed in green, some looked like glowing gold, and at least one had skin like black, polished marble. I took as many mental notes of their different appearances as I did when discovering the Kingdom Palace. One day, Breanadan and I were walking up to the Father's throne and standing in front of it was a bright, radiant spirit. He emitted a pure, white light which was different from the rich colors I had seen in the others. If Breanadan looked like an amethyst, then this spirit was like a diamond. As we walked up to him, Breanadan whispered to me, "He's a high prince."

It happened again some days later while I was standing with the three princes I had previously met. The pure, white light of this high prince entered the room and I could tell he carried a greater authority than the others. Since I was comfortable with Breanadan I said, "Someday you are going to have to explain to me how all this works. Who are the high princes? How many are there? How do Michael and Gabriel fit into all of this?" Apparently my conversation with Breanadan was overheard, and that bright, white angel exclaimed, "I'm Uriel!"

To put things in chronological order, I knew that there was an archangel named "Uriel," but not much more than that. I had read the book of Enoch some years before, but all I recalled was that this was a known name of a known archangel (or high prince). Yet here I was standing with him and the princes under his authority — and I didn't know the first thing to do or say. All I got out was a stunned, "Hi," but it didn't take Uriel long to put me at ease. He was as friendly as Breanadan and he seemed to have as much respect for me as I did for him. I'll get back to that shortly.

Once our introduction had been made we visited each other often, and he had a lot of insight to share. We talked about the structure of the heavens, the original state of Adam and Eve in the garden, the fall of man, and the importance of the stars and constellations. It would take a whole other book to talk about that last subject (and I plan to do just that), but suffice it to say, I learned a lot talking to him. Uriel is a revealer of mysteries, and his perspective is unique among all the other spirits I've met. It seems his job is to perceive the whole of the Kingdom, from the tops of the heavens to the bottoms of the earth. His grace to peer into the depth of creation is what makes him perfectly suited to explain the unexplainable.

After we had spent weeks getting to know each other in the Spirit, I finally looked around to see what, if anything, had been written about him. I found that his name means "Light of God," which seemed very fitting due to the pure, white radiance constantly surrounding him. Also, in the book of *Enoch* and the apocryphal book, *2 Esdras*, Uriel is seen revealing the secrets of the cosmos and answering life's questions — which was the same job he was doing with me.

Here's one thing Uriel told me that has stuck with me ever since. He said he liked being around me because I wouldn't worship him. When people start giving them the praise and devotion that is only appropriate for our heavenly Dad, it is like a stench in their nostrils. So it was refreshing for them to be enjoyed for who they really are without being repulsed by false worship. It's easy to see where people go the wrong way with this. It is awe-inspiring to be in the presence of radiant and majestic beings, but what if they feel the same way about us?

I can recall one visit to the Garden where it seemed I was the one inspiring awe. I was walking around with my heavenly Dad when, to my surprise, the angels I had grown to call friends had kneeled around me and bowed their heads. I don't have words for how uncomfortable that made me. Even Uriel was resting on one knee with his head down. The Lord and I were the only ones standing and He smiled as brightly as I have ever seen Him. However, I needed an immediate explanation before I labeled myself a heretic and had an official freak-out. By this time, I knew that Uriel was a high prince like Michael or Gabriel, so why would he bow to me? The Lord said to me, "Christopher, they see you as the king I have made you to be. You are ruling with My authority; and when they look at you, they see a son of God."

These must have been the scriptures they were thinking about when they bowed to me that day:

But when the fullness of the time came, God sent forth His Son, born of a woman, born under the Law, so that He might redeem those who were under the Law, that we might receive the adoption as sons. Because you are sons, God has sent forth

the Spirit of His Son into our hearts, crying, "Abba! Father!"
(Galatians 4: 4-6)

For the anxious longing of the creation waits eagerly for the
revealing of the sons of God. (Romans 8:19)

Even though this was a shocking moment, it was just one
more calculated step to get me to see reality. They all wanted me to know that I was a king, and they wanted me to
feel like it. In other words, they didn't bow to me to flatter
me. They bowed to me so that I would believe the truth.

CHAPTER 13

RECEIVING GIFTS

There is a lot of interest in the angels who protect us. The term, "guardian angel," has been around a long time for a reason. You learn pretty quickly here on planet earth that there are lots of things out there that can do you harm; so it's nice knowing that there are spirits around you charged with keeping you out of trouble. I met my guardian in those months traveling around the heavens with Breanadan. He was one of the nine powers that I met, and he was covered from head to toe in gleaming, silvery armor. He also wore a crimson cape on his back and he carried a spear and a shield. He was big, tall, and ready for battle; but it was our second meeting when I learned he was fighting on my behalf.

This may qualify as too much information, but he made that second visit while I was in the bathroom. Yes, it was as comical as it sounds. He stood right in front of me and said, "I'm Paladin, and I never leave you." With a grin I responded, "I can see that." All kidding aside, it was the perfect place to make that point. If I'm not alone in the bathroom, then I am never really alone. The last thing we talked about before he let me perceive I had some privacy was that I was free to call on him whenever I needed help.

In the last chapter I talked about learning to distinguish spirits by their color, but there were some other discernible traits

I was picking up as well. For instance, some spirits looked fiery, and they were typically perceived in colors of red and orange hues. Some looked like they were made of water, so that their skin had a blue, translucent quality. In Paladin's case there wasn't one specific color, and I couldn't see under that armor either. When I asked him what kind of spirit he was, he said he was a virtue. Here is a good definition of virtue: moral excellence; goodness; righteousness. Also, a virtue is a classification of angel in some of the traditional angelic hierarchies I mentioned before.

When I asked Paladin to tell me about the Virtues, he gave me things like love and patience as examples. He also said there were spirits tasked with radiating those qualities over people, places, or even cities. Apparently virtues make great guardians, too; because according to Paladin, they never loose a fight. I don't know about you, but a ten-foot tall, armor-clad virtue, who doesn't lose, sounded like a great guardian angel. One more fun fact — I had to look up the word "Paladin," just like I did after I learned Breanadan's name. It means "virtuous knight."

Here's another example of a name that had a specific meaning; only this time, it was the name of an animal. If you love animals, or any living thing for that matter, then you'll be right at home in heaven. In that realm, the relationship between mankind and all creatures is perfectly restored. So it is not unusual to have a bird fly right up on your shoulder and, I dare to say, look happy. In this case, Jesus and Breanadan wanted to give me a gift, so they presented to me a solid white eagle. I knew there was no such thing in the earth realm, but heaven does not have such limitations. I held the eagle on my shoulder and asked if he had a name. Jesus answered, "His name is Arnol." As you can guess, I searched for that name as soon as I was done walking in the Spirit. I quick Internet search revealed the meaning as "strength of the eagle." I wasn't surprised anymore when things like this would happen — but it never got old, either. As for Arnol, he became a constant companion in the Spirit. Rarely a day goes by that he doesn't swoop down and land on my shoulder as we explore the heavenly places.

God likes to give gifts to His kids. Some are the more intangible things like Uriel's insight into the mysteries, or Paladin's protection. But some are as touchable as a pet eagle or a crown. Let me give another example: To tell this story, I have to introduce one more ministering spirit. He was another one of the powers that served Breanadan, and he appeared to me in a translucent, yellow-green robe. It had gold hour glasses embroidered on the front, joined together in an intricate pattern from his shoulders down to his feet. He looked wispy, and he was the first spirit I had seen with four wings flowing out from his back. His specific area of authority was the time dimension, and he described it as just another current through which we move. To him, time had pathways just like the ones we know in our physical world; and they needed watching over, too. He gave me a tip about how his work is seen on planet earth: Have you ever bumped into someone unexpectedly and it seemed almost impossible to have arrived there at the same place and at just the right time? There might have been a spirit involved to make sure that chance meeting wasn't a chance at all.

He had a gift to give me as well — a gold pocket watch. When I opened it up, it was like no other clock I had ever seen. There were numerous hands, much more than was needed to tell the minutes and hours, and some even turned opposite the normal direction. I could make out the traditional functions of a watch, but I knew there was more to this device than just keeping a twenty-four hour schedule. You have to start somewhere though, so here is the first thing I learned it could do:

Like most people, I've used an alarm clock to get up in the morning — but I really don't like them. I find them to be abrupt and obnoxious. So when mine stopped working, I did not grieve at all. However, I needed a replacement, and that's when I wondered if the watch I had in the Spirit could work for me on earth. I asked the Lord about it, and He seemed thrilled that I was finally going to give it a try. Before I went to bed the next night, I went into the Spirit and opened up that gold pocket watch. I set the time (on the hands I recognized) for the time I wanted to wake up, then closed my eyes and went to bed. Sure enough, I was awake in my body the next morning at the right time. To this day, I have never gone back to a physical alarm clock because the spiritual watch just works better. It wakes me up more pleasantly, doesn't need batteries replaced, and is downright elegant in its construction. I don't think there is anything on this earth that can compare to its craftsmanship and functionality.

My most cherished possessions are the ones I have in the Spirit. They are eternal, beautiful, and a perfect fit for me.

But store up for yourselves treasures in heaven, where neither moth nor rust destroys, and where thieves do not break in or steal; for where your treasure is, there your heart will be also. (Matthew 6: 20-21)

CHAPTER 14

CITIES OF ANGELS

When you see something really amazing, it's hard to keep it to yourself. For instance, have you ever seen an extra special sunset and immediately pointed it out to those around you? Or have you come home from a vacation and invited your friends over to take them through a slide show of images? The desire to share those great pictures is always in the back of our minds, even while we're taking them. To prove this point, I had the chance to visit Glacier National Park as a college student and I think I took more pictures of that place than I did of all the places I had previously been, combined. When I got home, I put all the pictures in an album, and the only reason I have ever taken it out since then is to show it to someone who hasn't been there. I think it's beneficial to do this sort of thing with our heavenly journeys as well. If you've been on a fantastic trip, be it earthly or heavenly, you should feel free to share the pictures.

I'm going to do a little bit of that right now. Specifically, I'd like to share my visits to some different heavenly palaces. If you will remember from before, Breanadan introduced me to his family, which involved meeting two other princes and the high prince, Uriel. As a part of our introductions, they invited me to their respective homes, which were different from each other and seemed to reflect each prince's nature and purpose. But without a doubt, they were all palatial, beautiful structures.

One of the princes had a home that looked like it was made of water, and all around it was water as far as I could see. As you can imagine, the watery theme gave the whole place a blue color, and rising up from the center was a spire that reached up into large white, puffy clouds. At the top of that spire was a circular observation deck that gave me the feeling of standing in the clouds. It was all very fitting, because this prince's area of influence was the water, and not just the water in the oceans. Clouds are water too, just in condensed form. So his area of authority included most oceanic issues and even weather patterns. Everything about his palace reminded me of this with its smooth, fluid design, and water-like transparency.

A few days later, we visited Uriel's home, which was perched right in the middle of the cosmos. All around it I could see the stars and nebula in their bright colors. And even though the sky was velvety black, the palace itself radiated the same kind of light I always see shining out of Uriel. In contrast to the palace I just described, Uriel's home was the shape of an angular crown. The lines weren't fluid or smooth, but more like the sharp facets of a crystal. There was a central spire reaching up from the center, and around it was a circle of at least five other diamond-shaped towers. Also, in contrast to the other prince's home, this palace seemed to be made of light, and it stood like a beacon in the midst of the dark firmament. On the inside, it was a busy place. All the angels under Uriel's authority were coming and going, and I spent days exploring the ins and outs of this home. Always present in the background was a faint metallic tinkling sound, almost like little crystals ringing together the way wind chimes do.

It wasn't long after I visited Uriel's home that I was introduced to two more of the well-known archangels. The first was Gabriel, and as a show of hospitality, he took me to see his palace in the heavens as well. It was the largest angelic palace I had seen. In fact, it seemed more like a heavenly city. We approached it from a good distance away, which was the only way to get a good perspective of the shear size of the place. At the center of the complex stood a white citadel. I don't mean that word in any kind of a military context. But it was larger and higher than the structures around it, and it had a commanding presence. It had gradually sloping sides, like a white mountain among the surrounding buildings and pavilions. At the top was a large, smooth dome. Given my American upbringing, it reminded me of the capitol building in Washington, D.C.

The surrounding buildings were also a soft, white color, and the city was full of lush green gardens and waterfalls full of light-blue water. Pools of water separated the major structures, and connecting them all together was an intricate network of translucent walkways. Walking from building to building on those pathways gave the impression of walking on water. We approached the city on one of these see-through walkways, and I was having a hard time making my feet keep going. Some things in heaven just have a way of making you joyfully stupefied!

I was joined on this visit by my heavenly Dad, Uriel, Breanadan, and Gabriel. As we all walked along the main thoroughfare towards the central building, another spirit came from the city to greet us. He looked fiery and he was dressed in golds, yellows, and reds. The other angels made his introduction. It was the high prince, Michael, and he did the same thing the others had done when they wanted to press the issue of my royal adoption — he took a knee and bowed his head. It was still very uncomfortable, even though it had happened before. Part of my uneasiness was because his reputation preceded him. This was, after all, the great prince that is traditionally known as the commander of the Lord's armies. He even gets the honors of locking horns with the devil when the war in heaven is described in John's Revelation. All that is to say, I was expecting to meet a fierce warrior, but I soon learned there was much more to him than that. When Michael looked up at me from down on his knee, I could see a tear rolling down his face. It wasn't a sad tear, just one of inexpressible joy. He then said to me, "I am so honored that you're here. I've been waiting for these days with great anticipation." When he got up we all walked together towards the main palace where we were shown into a welcoming room, away from all the activity.

It was then that Michael turned to me and started asking me questions. He wanted to know what redemption meant to me and how I understood Jesus' sacrifice at the Cross. It's not that He didn't know what those things were; he just wanted to know my perspective. I answered as best I could, and he listened intently and nodded occasionally. I mentioned in the previous chapters all the generosity I had experienced, but this was the first time I felt like I was giving something back. It didn't seem like much, but I was happy to offer my human understanding of the redemption story. Maybe it was an example of the following scripture:

> *As to this salvation, the prophets who prophesied of the grace that would come to you made careful searches and inquiries, seeking to know what person or time the Spirit of Christ within them was indicating as He predicted the sufferings of*

Christ and the glories to follow. It was revealed to them that
they were not serving themselves, but you, in these things which
now have been announced to you through those who preached the
gospel to you by the Holy Spirit sent from heaven—things into
which angels long to look. (1 Peter 1: 10-12)

On my way out, I had to ask Gabriel about the size
of his palatial city. He confirmed to me what I had thought
when I first saw his white citadel. It was a capital city for the
angels. His palace is a heavenly gathering place, and one of
his specific roles in the Kingdom is to look after all the families of ministering spirits. On a personal note, it was one of
my favorite places to visit — and not just because it was so
grand. There was something about the lush gardens mixed
with white buildings and blue waterfalls that appealed to me,
so it was a place I immediately wanted to visit again. Thankfully, Gabriel is as welcoming as any angel I have met, and he
made it clear that his house was open anytime I wanted to visit.
That's not a special privilege just for me, either. I think they
are so encouraged when any believer makes the journey that
they pull out all the stops so that we will feel totally at home.

CHAPTER 15

CO-LABORING

There were immediate benefits to learning more about the angels. The first was purely relational. I have grown to love these spirits as I would any companion in the earthly realm, and I value our friendships dearly. At first that felt a little weird, but it wasn't long before I realized that my heavenly Dad loves Michael and Gabriel as much as He loves me. So appreciating my relationship with them was just one more thing I could share with the Father. The other benefits stemmed from knowing what each of them could do. Just to recap, we've talked about angels working with virtues like love and patience. We talked about a spirit who watches over the time dimension. And, just in the last chapter, I mentioned a prince that works with weather patterns. As I grew more familiar with each of them, and as I lost my fear of asking them to help me with things, I saw just how ready and willing they were to be of service. Here is one example regarding the weather.

One of my best friends was engaged to be married and he asked me to officiate at the wedding ceremony. They were to be married in downtown Baltimore, right in the heart of the city, and it was going to be a beautifully decorated, outdoor ceremony. However, the forecast for the day was afternoon showers and thunderstorms. It just so happened that the wedding was to begin at 5 o'clock, right in the middle of thunderstorm time. We all arrived a few hours early to help set up and make sure everyone knew what they were doing. As we made the final arrangements, the sky looked clear and gave us little concern. However, about thirty minutes before the bride was to make her entrance, the sky grew darker and darker.

We all kept going as planned. The wedding party came out, I made my opening remarks, and the musicians started to lead us in song. That's when the darkest of clouds rolled in and the wind picked up. The canopy over the bride and groom started swaying, and the groom was doing his best to keep it from falling over. And then, I felt the first raindrop hit me right on the nose. Like any minister worth his salt, I had already prepared an extremely quick ceremony that skipped right to the vows and got everyone officially married and out of the storm; but I wasn't ready to give up just yet.

As I stood out of sight while the music played, I made a quick heavenly phone call. I knew two spirits who were involved in the weather, so I asked for both of them by name. Immediately I saw them standing in front of me, and I said hurriedly, "We need help here right now!" One of them looked at me with a smile and said, "It will not rain." Then, they flew up to the surrounding buildings and stationed themselves. I watched in the Spirit as others joined them until the rooftops were full of angels, which made a beautiful backdrop to an already glorious occasion. Predictably, there were no more raindrops. The wind died down to a gentle breeze and a golden ray of sunshine lit up the canopy over the bride and groom for the rest of the ceremony. The dark clouds stayed where they were, held back on all sides by our spirit friends. After the couple said "I do" and the wedding party made their exit, I dismissed the crowd to the reception. Within seconds, the rain started and the wind rushed in. The canopy fell over and all the guests still outside made a rush for the reception hall. I chuckled to myself the whole time as I raced to get my things and get inside because I felt like my angelic friends were making a point to me. I think they wanted to show me just how involved they were, and how much they enjoyed it. So, for dramatic effect, they held back the storm just long enough for the wedding to happen, and not a second longer. I think they were chuckling a little, too.

Now, one might ask if the same thing would have happened if I had thrown up a generic prayer to heaven without any regard for the angels. My response is that I don't know. God is so good, and His grace in answering our prayers isn't based on our knowledge of the ministering spirits. In other words, He's not working on our behalf because we are a bunch of know-it-alls. Rather, in every season of Christian history, the Lord has taken the time to give us a fuller understanding of how He works. We know more about "how" to pray now than we did twenty or thirty years ago. Might this be just another facet of God's education for us? Could interacting with the angels — by name — be another way He enriches our experience with Him? To me, it's another thing He is restoring to His people; and like everything He gives to us, it has immediate and positive effects. In this case, knowing which angels are responsible for the weather made for a fun and faith-building wedding ceremony. But here's another way that process has worked out a little closer to home:

I have to travel a lot in order to talk to people about experiencing heaven in the Spirit, so I'm often separated from my wife and kids. I'm a little on the protective side, so I don't like being away from them. However, because I know their angels, I can always set up a meeting in the Spirit to hear how things are going at home while I'm away. I do this often when I'm gone, because there isn't always an appropriate time for a phone call. So when I make time to go to heaven, I ask for my children's angels to be present. Then we will have a chat about what's going on with the kids. Are they behaving? Any dangers on the horizon? Everyone feeling well? Once I get that real-time report, I can thank them for looking after my family so well, or if there's a problem, I can talk with the other ministering spirits about sending some help back home.

As a husband and father, I feel a certain responsibility for my family, and it gives me great comfort to interact with the celestial beings that watch over them without ceasing. Even when I'm home I still take time to talk with the spirits watching over my kids. Those angels know things that are going on with them that even a parent might miss, so their insight is appreciated. Knowing the angels such as the ones who are responsible for the weather or your kids' wellbeing can be a rich blessing. They are our partners in this journey, and each one has a special personality and gifting that they put to use for our good. Unfortunately, that can't be said for their counterparts, whom we know as fallen angels, devils, or demons.

CHAPTER 16

FALLEN ANGELS

I think we can learn a lot from the old fable of Jack and the Beanstalk. I know that myths and fables aren't exactly on par with the encyclopedia as a reference source, but there are still ways that they can prove helpful. For instance, imbedded in old myths and legends are some historical truths, although of course in a slightly dramatized version. If you look in the right place, or from the right perspective, you can perceive some issues that go right to the heart of the human condition. In some ways, they're even more accurate than a history book when it comes to explaining how we got to be where we are. Since it may have been a while since you've heard it, I'll recap the plot of Jack and the Beanstalk, and then we'll see how it might relate to our discussion of experiencing the heavenly places.

The story starts out with Jack and his widowed mother in dire financial straits. Having lost their last source of income, Jack goes to town to sell all that they have in order to have something to eat for dinner. In town, he meets a man with magic beans and Jack buys them immediately. When he gets home (minus food for dinner — with the exception of three measly beans), his mom throws them out the window in anger and sends Jack straight to bed. That night, the beans sprout in to a gigantic beanstalk all they way up into the sky, and Jack takes it upon himself to climb up and see where it goes. He climbs above the clouds and enters into a totally different land. It's there that he finds a house filled with treasures; and, unfortunately, the giant those treasures belong to. Lacking some moral fortitude, Jack steals some of the treasures, and eventually the giant takes notice. After a third burglary, the giant pursues Jack down the beanstalk to reclaim his possessions and put an end to Jack. Jack beats him to the ground and promptly chops the beanstalk down, killing the giant and protecting his new loot.

It's kind of a morally ambiguous story, so there isn't much of an ethics lesson to be learned here. However, what if this fable is really somehow talking about some ingrained human understandings of heaven and what might be up there? Take a look at some possible interpretations of the main events: First, the story tells of a whole other realm that Jack discovers above the clouds. In many ways it's just like the land he came from, with a physical house and physical treasures that he could take back down with him. That sounds a little like discovering the heavens as we've been talking about. Then, it's the treasures themselves that are worth taking a look at. Could some knowledge be ingrained in our human psyche about treasures in heaven that neither moth nor rust can destroy? And, finally, it's what Jack encounters up there that is noteworthy. He meets a giant who is bent on killing him and I think we all know what that might be an example of.

There are some verses in the Bible that make it very clear that there's something up there that doesn't like us. Here is one from Ephesians.

Put on the whole armor of God, that you may be able to stand against the wiles of the devil. For we do not wrestle against flesh and blood, but against principalities, against powers, against the rulers of the darkness of this age, against spiritual hosts of wickedness in the heavenly places. (Ephesians 6: 11-12 NKJV)

I wonder if the giant is a metaphor for those "principalities" and "hosts of wickedness in the heavenly places?" Also, notice the kinds of spiritual forces named in the above passage — principalities and powers. We know from the earlier chapter that the archangel Michael is called a prince, and we know that the princes referenced above (principality just means prince) are not good princes. So these wicked principalities must be the same type of angel as Michael, but they're playing for the other team. In other words, lots of different kinds of angels have fallen from their holy and perfected state. They are still working in the same capacity as they were before, only now they are opposed to us instead of working for our good. You can see how Michael, Gabriel, Breanadan, Uriel, and the various powers serving with them all have their counterparts trying to fulfill an opposite and wicked purpose. Keep that in the back of your mind; we'll come back to it later.

Here's where Jack's story might hit a little more close to home. When people start realizing the free gift of intimacy and access to their heavenly Father in the Spirit, they start climbing up the beanstalk – so to speak. However, waiting for them in the space between the earth realm and heavenly realm is something bent on kicking them right back down to earth and keeping them ignorant of any life beyond the earthly, temporal one. So as believers start their journey up to the heavens, they feel this opposition. Sometimes it's totally unconscious;

but most people know that when they start reaching up for the Lord, all of hell seems to take notice and make things miserable. But it's Jack's response to the opposition that's really telling and perhaps indicative of our own earthly attitude. Jack cuts the beanstalk down in order to save himself, thus severing any connection he had to that other world. Out of self-preservation he gets away from the giant the only way he knew how; but it cost him his access to the treasures above the clouds.

There are lots of believers out there who have experienced a taste of heaven. Maybe they started on this journey but, just like Jack, they encountered something up there that was frightening and oppressive. So in order to maintain their normal lives, they back out altogether. Symbolically, they sever the beanstalk, and they try to forget that they ever had access to the heavenly realms. It doesn't surprise me at all that this condition is so ingrained in our collective human minds that the idea makes it into an old fable. However, what if Jack's story went a little differently? What if his meeting with the giant didn't end in his running for his life and ending the connection to heaven? What if Jack knew he had a right to be there — and it's the giant who has to leave?

The big reason the dark angels don't want us coming up there is this: They know that if we start to spend our time in the heavens, we'll realize we were born for it. And we'll realize that, from that perspective (or from that "height"), we can really mess up their plans. So they try to discourage us as quickly and as aggressively as possible. That's why some of the strongest opposition you will ever face is when you are taking your first steps into the heavenly realm. With that in mind, let me tell you about the first time I met a giant.

(In case you're wondering, he didn't say "Fee Fi Fo Fum!")

One evening, just a few months after all this started with me, I was having a hard time journeying in the Spirit. I had been practicing long enough to know that some days were just harder than others; but it seemed a little more challenging than usual. As per my usual routine, I had found a quiet spot to pray; and as I sat and looked with the eyes of my heart, I couldn't seem to focus on anything. It was like someone in my head had the T.V. remote and kept changing the channel over and over. I was getting frustrated just watching image after image pass by, and I was just about to give up and go to bed. I asked the Lord for help one last time, and that's when the picture suddenly snapped into focus.

I saw myself standing in the blackness of space; and a short distance away, I could see a bright, golden door. However, standing there between me and that door was a dark figure. He was tall and imposing — and by tall, I mean about fifty feet tall! That qualifies as "giant." He was the source of my discomfort and frustration, and I had the sense that the whole time I had been trying to look into the heavens, he was blocking my way and sending out a bunch of white noise to confuse me. I asked the Lord what he was and I heard the soft voice of the Father say, "principality." He was one of the fallen princes, and it was his job that night to stand in my way to the heavens.

I could see Jesus standing to my right — and He didn't look worried at all (as you can imagine). He just turned to me and simply asked, "What do you want him to do?" I said, "I just want him to get out of the way so I can go through that gold door." I didn't know where that door led, but in my brief experience at this point I knew that golden doors in the heavens led to cool things. So as soon as I had answered Jesus, the dark prince stepped to the side and stood motionless. It was an almost robotic move, as if he had no control over his actions. With the way open before me, I began to walk with my Lord to that gold door. As we passed by the imposing prince, I kept glancing at him because I thought he might reach out and slap me at any moment. But he just stood like a frozen statue as I walked by and went through that door into the courts of the Lord.

As I said earlier, the fallen angels don't want us up there because our activity really messes up their plans. When we are walking with Jesus in heaven, we are in the very dimension that those wicked spirits move around in. Remember, the Apostle Paul said they were in the heavenly places. That doesn't mean they get to roam around the throne room or anything like that. They just occupy the space directly above us. To put it another way, they are between us and our heavenly home. But consider this: When you are walking in the courts of the Lord with the Father, you observe them below you. That's right, you can look down on them, which is the exact position they work so hard to keep you from realizing. It is their worst case-scenario for believers to live and move in the heavenly realms.

When I saw that first principality, I was worried. Could he hurt me? Could he keep me from walking in the heavens? It's natural to feel like they're big, and we're small, and that means we are at a disadvantage. But all it took was one honest statement of what I wanted him to do, and he did it without protest. Over the years, I have encountered other wicked spirits. Some I have bumped into just like the scenario I described before, and others I have been sent to confront. I'll share some of those encounters in the next chapter. But what I learned from this first taste of heavenly warfare is that there is an effortless authority in dealing with the fallen angels when you keep climbing up the "beanstalk." Once you climb past their home and into your eternal citizenship, you can look down and see what they're planning. Then, you can talk with your heavenly Dad and see what He wants them to do. Maybe you just need to tell them to get out of the way. Or maybe they need to know that you're not going to climb back down and sever your connection to heaven just because they seem menacing and foreboding.

In other words, learn the lesson from the fable: People have been staying out of heaven because they don't want to deal with the dark spirits. And that's exactly the way those devils want it. I think it's time for a change.

CHAPTER 17

WICKED ASSEMBLIES

One day while I was hanging out with Jesus in the Spirit, he sent me on a little errand. He introduced me to an angel, who then took my hand as we flew out into the cosmos. We came to a dark tunnel that led straight down, and I wasn't sure I wanted to see where it led. There wasn't anything inviting about it. In every way, it was a sharp contrast to the rich colors and warm presence of the courts of the Lord. But down we went anyway, and I just kept an eye on my guide to make sure I didn't loose my way. After a long descent, we reached the bottom and started walking towards a structure that looked like an ancient coliseum. It sounded like any arena does on the day of a sporting event, with voices and commotion filling the air. The angel and I came to one of the entrances and started to peak inside, but we made sure to keep out of view. It sort of felt like spying.

What I saw on the inside was straight out of a horror movie. There were rows and rows of stands filled with ghastly, decaying creatures, and all of them were cheering. Their "master of ceremonies," so to speak, was standing in a balcony overlooking the coliseum floor, urging them on into an uproar. Then I could see what they were getting so excited about. Out of another entrance, dozens of grim spirits entered the coliseum, carrying a statue-replica of Jesus. They brought it to the center of the arena and began hurling insults and throwing things. The MC in the balcony kept goading them on, and the mocking reached a crescendo. I was actually stunned by the absurdity of it all. First, the statue wasn't Jesus. It was just a replica, and a poor one at that. But the devils in that coliseum didn't care. They kept flinging insults at it like it was the real person of Jesus who could hear and feel their hatred. Then of course there's the obvious shocking truth: They hate him so much that they take time out of their day to get together and curse a statue of Him. That's a lot of hatred.

As you can guess, the angel and I were unwelcome guests at their blasphemy party, and they soon found us out and led us to the arena floor. It's good to point out here that even though I was surrounded by decaying spirits, I wasn't scared. I'm not sure if it was knowing that an angel was with me, or maybe the fact that it was Jesus' idea to send me there, but something gave me confidence that I would be okay. The devil in charge of the whole soiree (the one getting everyone in a frenzy) looked down from his balcony and demanded to know what we were doing there. He was upset for sure; and if a devil's face could get red with anger, his was doing just that as he yelled at us. He was particularly upset with the angel who brought me there, and he said things to him like, "You should know better than to be here!"

That's when the angel shrugged his shoulders and gave me a little wink and a nod. Then, looking up to the balcony and motioning to me he said, "I'm with him." I gave the angel a stunned look and in a hushed voice said, "Wait... I thought I was with you!" It was a funny, double-take kind of moment because I thought he was there to show me the ropes — and now he was shirking the responsibility of crashing their party and putting the focus squarely on me. That wasn't desirable considering what I had just witnessed. But the smile on the angel's face told me that I had nothing to worry about. So I looked up to the balcony and demanded an answer of my own. "What are you doing here?" I asked. I think the creature was shocked that I didn't cower to him, and he had that same robotic response I described with the fallen prince in the last chapter. He answered me because he didn't have any choice in the matter. It's as if his lips moved even if he didn't want them to. And this was his answer: "We come here to practice blasphemy. This is our entertainment, and it keeps the other fallen spirits from being discouraged in their work. If we didn't do this, then they might not be as committed to their rebellion."

I responded in a simple, matter-of-fact tone, "Well, you can't just keep doing this here. You have to stop your blasphemy party." His face got red again and he huffed off his balcony perch and started shouting obscenities. All around in the stands, the fallen spirits started to leave. It happened without any violence or drama, but with a tangible sense of resignation, as if they knew they had to leave and there was simply no use in fighting it. Before I knew it, the coliseum was empty; and the angel and I made our way back up the dark tunnel and into the courts of the Lord. Jesus was waiting for me when I got back, and he smiled as He asked me what happened. Of course He already knew, but He was excited that I got to experience another effortless victory. Between meeting the dark principality I described in the last chapter and crashing this wicked party, I was starting to realize that I had a lot to be confident about in the Spirit. If you will recall, when I saw the big, dark principality, I was worried he might hurt me as I walked passed him. And certainly there were moments in this coliseum when I wondered if I would get out okay. But one thing was resounding in me — when I'm up here in the Spirit, I can't be hurt, I can't be killed, and I'm already living the eternal life. So what is there to be afraid of?

Here are a few more things worth gleaning from this experience. First, visiting the dark coliseum was a lot like going to Gabriel's or Breanadan's home. It was a gathering place for spirits, albeit obviously fallen ones. So they have homes, too, and their dwelling places reflect what they have become. They aren't glorious, colorful, structures. They're dark, monochrome, and you have to go down to get there. The angel and I took a long descent in that tunnel, but I never had the sense I was leaving the heavens. It's the same principal the apostle Paul spoke of. Those wicked spirits reside in the heavenly places; just not the highest heavens that hold the throne rooms and palaces of the Lord. Lastly, dealing with these wicked spirits is a normal part of experiencing all of the heavenly places. It's nothing to be afraid of, and it's nothing to worry about. Even if you have to go to their home and crash their blasphemy party, try to remember that about 2,000 years ago, the Apostle Paul made it pretty clear that dealing with them was our job.

CHAPTER 18

WAR IN HEAVEN

I went to meet a friend at a coffee shop one day. When I got there, I decided to sit outside and wait for him to show up. It was a stormy afternoon, with lots of low, dark clouds rolling quickly by. The atmosphere was charged with nature's energy, and I enjoyed watching the lightning and listening to the thunder. Since I had a few minutes to wait, I started to peek open the eyes of my heart and see what was going on in the Spirit. The first thing I noticed was a familiar presence sitting next to me, easily identified by his bright, white aura. It was Uriel, and I couldn't help chuckling at the fact that I was sitting at a major coffee shop chain with the archangel, Uriel. Sometimes, the truth really is stranger than fiction. So there we sat together, enjoying a little chat while I sipped my coffee.

He encouraged me to look around at everything and to try to see the earthly realm and the heavenly realm at the same time. The coffee shop was right on a busy road, with a strip mall directly across the way, so there was a lot going on in the earth realm. When I started to look with both sets of eyes, I could see the sky full of spirits coming and going. Some were holy and some were fallen. In both realms, the environment looked like a busy thoroughfare. I watched spirits move along with the dark clouds rolling overhead, but my attention was drawn down to a fallen spirit standing on the side of the road. He was dressed in a black overcoat, and he looked like the kind of guy who would pick a fight with anyone just for the fun of it. He watched the cars drive by, one by one, as if looking for a ride. Uriel noticed him, too, and we talked about him for a minute. Turns out, he was trying to hitch-hike. His assignment was to put out little tendrils of anger and discord to the cars passing by, and if someone took the bait and started arguing, then he would ride home with them. Uriel didn't give him a chance to find a ride at that moment, though, because he called him over to join us at our table.

This was another moment when I was tempted to worry. The dark figure walked across the street to where we were sitting and he had a smirk on his face that was unsettling. I had to remind myself that no matter what this guy pulls, there's an archangel sitting next to me, so I was pretty sure the wicked spirit was out-ranked. Now, just to set the scene, there were people sitting all around me as I had my "unseen" conversation with Uriel. However, when the fallen angel arrived at our table, he started to affect them in tangible ways. As soon as he sat down, the young couple next to me suddenly jumped out of their chairs. They were startled because a black widow spider had crawled out of its hiding space next to their table. In a frenzy, they looked for a way to kill it while I just watched the fallen spirit smirk at me from across the table. When he showed up, his foul presence called to the dark, venomous things surrounding us, which made the black widow scurry into motion. After the young man had dis-patched the spider, they collected their things and left. The wicked angel got up as well, saying, "Well, they're my ride."

Like any good Christian, I immediately thought of

ways to oppose this spirit. I was sure the young couple didn't need his influence that night. As he was leaving, I turned to Uriel and said, "Aren't you going to have a battle royale right here and stop him from going with them?" Up until now, I haven't mentioned what warfare looks like between spirits. I had a taste of how I might be used in a struggle against wickedness in the heavens, but I had not seen angel on angel combat. And I wouldn't on this occasion, either. However, my question prompted a lesson about spiritual warfare (and that's probably why Uriel invited the fallen angel over in the first place). I guess I always thought that angels fought like humans did, with the two sides duking it out until one side permanently vanquished the other. It may seem a little silly, but I had this picture of Uriel dealing a death-blow to his foe and standing victoriously over him with his foot on the fallen angel's neck. But Uriel didn't do that. He didn't even lift a finger to stop him. Rather, he took the next few minutes to explain some things to me:

First, he said that he doesn't fight just any fallen spirit that crosses his path. When angels from heaven are going about their business, they bump into their counterparts that fell from perfection. When they meet, they wrestle, since they are assigned to the same space, people, or event. We saw this in the chapter about Daniel and the angels. The fallen prince hovering over Persia was in a wrestling match with another prince, Michael. It was a prince wrestling with another prince. So, in that context, it would have seemed a bit strange if the archangel Uriel entered into a struggle with a devil that seemed far, far below his stature and rank. If Uriel were to throw down with someone, it would likely be a wicked prince — not an annoying hitchhiker.

Next, Uriel pointed out that unlike human warfare,

angelic combat does not end with one of them dying. They are, after all, eternal spirits. So there aren't any less spirits roaming around the Kingdom today (holy or not) then there were since creation. In other words, all of the spiritual battles that have taken place since Satan started the rebellion (and there have been many) have not reduced the angelic population at all. Simply put, their warfare does not involve killing each other. Rather, it is a struggle to establish authority so that the work of the Kingdom keeps moving forward.

Now, going back to my role in all of this, I wondered what I should do to help protect the young couple leaving with the dark hitchhiker. Should I tell him to get out of their way like I did to the fallen principality? When I expressed this to Uriel, he said, "Where would you send him? If he doesn't get in the car with them, he'll go right back to the street looking for a ride." I countered, "What if I send him far away?" Uriel replied, "Then, he'll look for people to attach himself to in that place." As a last resort I thought, "Can't I send him to the pit? Isn't that a place that spirits are held in prison?" Uriel answered, "The pit is for the angels that rebelled in the days of Noah." In case you're wondering, that's in keeping with the scriptures. Take a look at these verses:

> *For if God did not spare angels when they sinned, but cast them into hell and committed them to pits of darkness, reserved for judgment; and did not spare the ancient world, but preserved Noah, a preacher of righteousness, with seven others, when He brought a flood upon the world of the ungodly (2 Peter 2:4-5)*

> *For Christ also died for sins once for all, the just for the unjust,*

so that He might bring us to God, having been put to death in
the flesh, but made alive in the spirit; in which also He went
and made proclamation to the spirits now in prison, who once
were disobedient, when the patience of God kept waiting in the
days of Noah, during the construction of the ark, in which a
few, that is, eight persons, were brought safely through the water.
(1 Peter 3: 18-20)

So if there wasn't a place to send them where they couldn't in-
terfere with people, what would happen if I didn't do anything?

Uriel explained it this way: On the ride home from
the coffee shop, the fallen angel would try to incite an argu-
ment. If successful, he would stay with that couple as long
as they gave in to his particular brand of wickedness. If he
stayed for a while, he might even bring some of his friends
who are bigger and darker to try to keep them away from
their heavenly Dad. If, however, they don't take the bait on
the way home, then he will have to leave them. In that case,
he would come right back to his spot on the road looking for
a ride. If no one gives in to his influence, he'll become idle,
and eventually have to report back to his superiors. "His superiors don't want him to be idle," Uriel said. He said it in a
tone of voice that implied there would be some punishment
for him before he was sent back out to do his wicked job.

I still wasn't convinced that I should do nothing. So I
asked the archangel, "What are my options?" Uriel answered,
"Pray for the couple." So, I did. I asked for their spirits to respond to the Father's love and that they would have the fortitude to resist the fallen spirit's attack. Now, before we move on,
let me make a few disclaimers: This was not a chapter about re-

defining how we think of spiritual warfare or a manual on deliverance. It is one glimpse into the world of the holy and fallen angels — and I hope it gives a fuller view of how things work in their realm. There have been other times when I was asked to send fallen spirits out of people's lives; and in the last chapter, I mentioned clearing out a whole coliseum of fallen angels. Also, Jesus, Himself, made of habit of casting evil spirits out of people. So clearly it's okay to send them away. Ultimately, I don't think Uriel brought all this up to teach me about casting out devils.

I think he was echoing the same principals we can find in Apostle Paul's letter to the Ephesian church. Here is one of the relevant passages:

> To me, the very least of all saints, this grace was given, to preach to the Gentiles the unfathomable riches of Christ, and to bring to light what is the administration of the mystery which for ages has been hidden in God who created all things; so that the manifold wisdom of God might now be made known through the church to the rulers and the authorities in the heavenly places. (Ephesians 3: 9-10)

If it's our job to make the whole wisdom of God known to all the heavenly rulers (another way to say principalities), then we might want to develop our sensitivity to their world. And we might want to be aware of the aspects of God's manifold wisdom that He wants to display. It might be different in each situation. On this particular day, it wasn't my job to cast the devil out. There wasn't a place I could send him where he would be out of everyone's hair. He was going to bother someone that night, so it made more sense to pray for the people than to send the spirit out into the Atlantic ocean — where I'm sure he would have probably found some shipping lanes to prowl.

In the Palaces of Heaven

CHAPTER 19

THE DARK TOWER TO HEAVEN

Have you noticed that when someone brings up traveling around heaven in the Spirit, it immediately conjures up thoughts of the New Age movement? There's a good reason for that. Just go check out your local bookstore. There are shelves of books about talking to spirit guides and projecting oneself into the spiritual realm. So as you've been reading this testimony, you might have thought to yourself that this is very dangerous ground. For instance, what if you start journeying to heaven and begin listening to the wrong voices? What if you end up totally deceived because you played with something you were never supposed to touch? What if the fallen princes and devils are just too much to handle? These are all wise questions any discerning Christian (told to "test the spirits") should ask. What I find interesting, though, is that in the last chapter we read a quote from the Apostle Paul concerning our job as the church. Did you notice it centered directly on the heavenly places? However, all it takes to back out of that commission is a refusal of anything unseen, or a belief that any journey into the Spirit is wrought with so much danger that it's not worth the risk.

The fallen angels have done a good job of scaring believers away from a true spiritual journey while tricking vulnerable and rebellious people into dangerous spiritual encounters, encouraging them to dive right in. The truth is, they want people going up to heaven, but under one, specific condition: They want humans experiencing heaven on their (the fallen spirits') terms. They want to be the ones we find when we discover our access to the other realms (and don't forget they can disguise themselves as "angels of light" as part of the illusion and seduction). They want to be the ones speaking to us, leading us, and controlling us. And they would love it if we decided to worship them (or ourselves!)...

The last thing they want is for people to go to heaven and find the Father sitting in His courts, welcoming His children into their inheritance. So if you don't do it on their terms, they go back to being the giant trying to chase Jack down the beanstalk. But, if you're willing to play their game, they'll do their best to make it seem like it's in your best interest. They promise power and indulgence of all our self-centered, power-seeking natures, all while exploiting an ingrained human desire to rediscover our connection to heaven. And they've been doing this for a long, long time. It's called witchcraft, or the occult, and it's been around since the first book of the Bible. Let's take a look at *Genesis, chapter 11*, to see this process at work.

> *Now the whole earth used the same language and the same*
> *words. It came about as they journeyed east, that they found*
> *a plain in the land of Shinar and settled there. They said*
> *to one another, "Come, let us make bricks and burn them*
> *thoroughly." And they used brick for stone, and they used tar*
> *for mortar. They said, "Come, let us build for ourselves a city,*
> *and a tower whose top will reach into heaven, and let us make*
> *for ourselves a name, otherwise we will be scattered abroad over*
> *the face of the whole earth." The Lord came down to see the*

city and the tower which the sons of men had built. The Lord said, "Behold, they are one people, and they all have the same language. And this is what they began to do, and now nothing which they purpose to do will be impossible for them. Come, let Us go down and there confuse their language, so that they will not understand one another's speech." (Genesis 11: 1-7)

Sometime in the 3rd millennium B.C., mankind got together and built a tower; and the tower's sole purpose was to reach into the heavens. Now, it would be really easy for us to look at this story and say, "Poor, uneducated, bronze-age man, didn't you know that heaven isn't high up in the sky?" Can you imagine a modern scientist being there and trying to tell them that there's over 100,000 feet of atmosphere above them, and after that it's the blackness of space, and that there simply isn't a "height" you can achieve that will get you to heaven? But I don't think these were uneducated, naive people. And I don't think they even thought that altitude was the key to reaching the heavenly realms. I think they were going to do something on that tower that would open up the door to the other realms — and a quick look at historical context might prove that point.

Did you know that just a few hundred years prior to the engineering project at Babel, a group of angels fell from God's grace, came to earth, and began corrupting mankind? Did you know that those fallen angels were responsible for teaching man certain technological advancements, and also for producing hybrid offspring? The basics of that story are covered in *Genesis 6*, and the details are in the apocryphal book, Enoch. Those hybrid offspring were half angel, half man; and their existence grieved the Lord so much, it moved Him to destroy the earth in a flood. The Bible calls them the Nephilim, or giants, or men of renown. (*Genesis 6:4*) It's hard to imagine that world, but it did exist. It was a time when fallen angels intermingled with humans in an overt and substantial manner. They were so present and tangible that they were even reproducing with human women, and their unnatural children were the subjects of many myths and legends passed down in different cultures. And it all occurred right before the tower of Babel. To put it in context, that world was historically closer to the tower builders than the American Revolution is for us today. Or, to use another historical marker, the Nephilim were as recent a memory for them as the American civil war would be to us.

It would be a big misconception to think the tower was a vain or pointless project, undertaken by ignorant people. It's completely possible that those folks knew more about how the world really works than we do today, given that they lived in a time we can't even adequately describe — except as mythological. That's a convenient way to say we have no idea how a world like that would work, and we have no categories to explain how that's feasible. So could it be possible that the people building the tower weren't so ignorant? Might they have known it was possible to reach into the heavens? Could it be that they built the tower on principals we don't know anything about but that were completely effective for its designed purpose? Again, I'm not talking about the tower physically "reaching heaven"… I'm talking about what would happen upon or with that tower.

If we have any doubts about whether it would have worked, just take a look at the Lord's response to them. He says, "And this is what they began to do, and now nothing which they purpose to do will be impossible for them." Notice the Lord says that nothing will be impossible for them — now. Before they built the tower, they all had the same language; and yet that didn't enable them to do whatever they wanted. So if their unity wasn't to blame for the sudden ability to accomplish anything, what could it be? The thing that changed was that they were going to start accessing the heavenly places on top of that tower and that would allow them to achieve anything. But the Lord knew they were not ready for it.

I wouldn't be surprised if they learned how to access heaven from the very fallen angels we were just talking about. Those wicked spirits would want nothing more than for man to open the doors into the heavenly realms on their terms (again, the wicked spirits' terms), so that they could keep influencing mankind's development. Even if the original Nephilim were all wiped out in the flood (and that's doubtful, the Bible says they were around after the flood, too), there was still a recent memory of their activity. Mankind learned the occult practices from the fallen ones (and all of the occult is from the fallen ones no matter what deceptive notions are prevalent about that topic). And once the genie is out of the bottle, it's hard to get it back in. Here's the bottom line: Whatever the people were going to do on that tower was going to work, otherwise there was no reason for the Lord to stop them. And they were going to do it in a way that was not sanctioned by the Father. That only leaves occult methods and practices as probable means of reaching heaven.

If you're connecting the dots, you can see what the fallen angels have been doing for the last 4,000 years or so. They want people to open the door to heaven, but, again, on their terms. Those devils know that it's powerful, which is why so many people are drawn to the occult. If it didn't work, no one would do it. A lesson we could learn from the tower of Babel, then, is that it's possible to reach into the heavens without the Father's blessing and protection. That raises the question, what would have happened if God hadn't stopped them?

God is holy, pure, and incorruptible. The highest heavens, which contain His throne rooms, courts, and palaces are equally incorruptible. We could say that they are eternal places, because they don't rust or decay. God's glory is inseparable from these eternal places; so being in the highest heavens is to be in His glory. In contrast, when Adam fell in the beginning of *Genesis*, he became corrupted. It took a while (over 900 years), but his body did die. He fell from the glory he knew in the Garden, and every generation after him seemed to fall farther and farther away. And even if Adam or his descendants wanted to go back to the perfect garden, they couldn't. It was now off-limits. If we can extrapolate here, we can see how the glorious, eternal garden and the glorious, eternal heavens might be one and the same. And the point relevant to us is that they were both off-limits. God had a plan to change that, and we'll get to that in a minute. But for now, let's look back at Babel to see what could have happened.

If man had been successful and opened the door into the heavens, he could only have gone so far. The highest heavens, that we just talked about, were closed to the sinful. That means the ones on the top of the tower could not have entered the courts of the Lord and found safety in the Father's presence. They could have only accessed those parts of heaven being occupied by the fallen angels. Think back, again, to the verse in *Ephesians 6*. The tower of Babel would have opened a door to heaven, but only to the waiting arms of the hosts of wickedness in the heavenly places. That would have been a re-run of the pre-flood days that nobody in their right mind would want to watch. The quality of life before the flood was horrible. It was violent, wicked, and the vast majority of the blame could be placed on the Nephilim. Humans were oppressed by the giants; and the last thing the Lord wanted was for humanity to suffer the same fate again. But, as humans, we have a tradition of being slow to learn from our history and our mistakes, and so the tower seemed like a good idea.

Our heavenly Father was actually moved with loving protection for his children when he confused the language at Babel and scattered the people across the earth. In that moment, God was a father watching his child run out into the street without seeing the oncoming car. The Father did what any parent would have done. He ran out into the street and snatched the child out of harms way. To the child, it may have looked harsh; but the child didn't see the danger lurking in the road. Confusing the language was a bold move, and it makes us consider just how dangerous the tower at Babel could have been.

Chapter 20

A Way Back In

God never intended to keep the perfect garden and the glorious heavens off-limits. In fact, the whole story of the Bible, from start to finish, is the story of God re-affirming his relationship with mankind and re-establishing man in a position of glory and perfection. It is a redemption story. Therefore, the lesson we need to learn from the tower of Babel is not that God didn't want people to know the heavenly realms; He just didn't want them to do it the wrong way. Or to put it differently, God didn't want man to access the heavens until He had made him ready for it. God proved this to His people over and over again when He kept showing them the connection between the heavens and the earth. It was His way of saying, "Friends, I'm not trying to keep you out, I just have to restore you so that you can come up here and be with me!" God did it in subtle and not-so-subtle ways; but all of them are examples of God revealing the connection to heaven — not holding it back. Our first example comes from Jacob's famous dream:

> *Then Jacob departed from Beersheba and went toward Haran.*
> *He came to a certain place and spent the night there, because*
> *the sun had set; and he took one of the stones of the place and*
> *put it under his head, and lay down in that place. He had a*
> *dream, and behold, a ladder was set on the earth with its top*

reaching to heaven; and behold, the angels of God were ascending and descending on it. (Genesis 28: 10-12)

Remember, Abraham and his descendants, Isaac and Jacob, weren't that far removed from the tower of Babel and the pre-flood world. Jacob would have grasped the significance of the dream, and known that this was not a metaphoric ladder to heaven. There was an actual connection. Also, I see the classic Jack and the beanstalk fable again. There's not much difference between a beanstalk going to the heavenly realms and a ladder. Humanity has always known, even if it was in the back of our collective minds, that you could go up to the heavens.

Some generations later, God calls Moses to lead His people out of Egypt; and here we find a not-so-subtle reminder of the connection. Here are the scriptures that describe it:

Then they set out from Succoth and camped in Etham on the edge of the wilderness. The Lord was going before them in a pillar of cloud by day to lead them on the way, and in a pillar of fire by night to give them light, that they might travel by day and by night. He did not take away the pillar of cloud by day, nor the pillar of fire by night, from before the people. (Exodus 13: 20-22)

Then the cloud covered the tent of meeting, and the glory of the Lord filled the tabernacle. Moses was not able to enter the tent of meeting because the cloud had settled on it, and the glory of the Lord filled the tabernacle. Throughout all their journeys whenever the cloud was taken up from over the tabernacle, the sons of Israel would set out; but if the cloud was not taken up,

then they did not set out until the day when it was taken up.
For throughout all their journeys, the cloud of the Lord was on
the tabernacle by day, and there was fire in it by night, in the
sight of all the house of Israel. (Exodus 40: 34-38)

You can imagine being in Israel's camp with the pillar of cloud
and fire reaching up into the sky. It would have looked like
a cosmic rope connecting the earthly realm to the heavenly
one. I think that to every Hebrew living at that time there
must have been some recognition that God was connecting
them to heaven. In this case, He was showing that this people, the whole nation of Israel, was joined to heaven. Maybe
they even connected the dots and considered this another step
in discovering God's way of accessing the heavenly realms.
Let's fast-forward to Jesus' ministry. There, in the gospels, we can
find another affirmation of a connection between the realms:

Six days later Jesus took with Him Peter and James and John
his brother, and *led them up on a high mountain by them-
selves. And He was transfigured before them; and His face
shone like the sun, and His garments became as white as light.
And behold, Moses and Elijah appeared to them, talking with
Him. Peter said to Jesus, "Lord, it is good for us to be here; if
You wish, I will make three tabernacles here, one for You, and
one for Moses, and one for Elijah." While he was still speak-
ing, a bright cloud overshadowed them, and behold, a voice out
of the cloud said, "This is My beloved Son, with whom I am
well-pleased; listen to Him!" When the disciples heard this,
they fell face down to the ground and were terrified. And Jesus
came to them and touched them and said, "Get up, and do not

be afraid." *(Matthew 17: 1-7)*

Jesus brought the heavenly and the earthly together on top of the mountain, and the Hebrew disciples probably thought back to Moses and the tabernacle when they saw the "bright cloud." Only now the connection to the heavens wasn't a grand phenomenon occurring over an entire nation. It was centered on the person of Jesus. This was a big moment in the story of our restoration to heaven. It showed us that the bond between heaven and earth was centered on a man. If we needed further proof, we can look back to something Jesus said about Himself, earlier in the gospels:

> *Nathaniel answered Him, "Rabbi, You are the Son of God; You are the King of Israel." Jesus answered and said to him, "Because I said to you that I saw you under the fig tree, do you believe? You will see greater things than these." And He said to him, "Truly, truly, I say to you, you will see the heavens opened and the angels of God ascending and descending on the Son of Man." (John 1: 49 – 51)*

Now we've come full circle, all the way back to Jacob's dream. If you look back there, you'll see the angels ascending and descending on a ladder that connects the earth to the heavens. In this last excerpt, we find Jesus quoting the same phrase; but instead of a ladder, the angels are traveling on the "Son of Man." This would have been a revelation to anyone following the story of God's people from Genesis all the way to the gospels. The connection to heaven — the door to the other realms — had always been Jesus. This is a far cry from the efforts of the citizens of Babel. They built a whole structure for their misguided occult practices. And maybe there's a lesson there about how much work is involved when we try to circumvent God. At the tower of Babel, mankind was trying to breach the door to the heavens on its own. So they had to align themselves with the same dark spiritual forces that ruined the world before the flood.

You can imagine God watching them and saying, "Please, just wait! I have a plan to get you back up here with Me. But you need to see the rest of the story! I'm going to bridge the gap with My Son, and He will show you the way to the heavenly realms!"

CHAPTER 21

TOWERS OF LIGHT

Jesus' followers had seen Him transfigured on the mountain; and they had seen him do miracle after miracle on the way to His death and resurrection. And during that time, the Lord made some special promises to the believers. We touched on it before, in the introduction. He told them that something better was coming, and He reminds them of it right before He ascends to Heaven.

> ...but you will receive power when the Holy Spirit has come upon you; and you shall be My witnesses both in Jerusalem, and in all Judea and Samaria, and even to the remotest part of the earth." (Acts 1: 6-8)

So after Jesus translated to the heavenly realms, they all waited for the promise to be fulfilled. It happens, here, in the second chapter of Acts:

> When the day of Pentecost had come, they were all together in one place. And suddenly there came from heaven a noise like a violent rushing wind, and it filled the whole house where they were sitting. And there appeared to them tongues as of fire distributing themselves, and they rested on each one of them. And they were all filled with the Holy Spirit and began to speak

with other tongues, as the Spirit was giving them utterance.
Now there were Jews living in Jerusalem, devout men from every
nation under heaven. And when this sound occurred, the crowd
came together, and were bewildered because each one of them
was hearing them speak in his own language. (Acts 2: 1-6)

This was the moment that changed everything. It marked the beginning of life with the Holy Spirit, and I don't think there is any way to overstate its significance. I bet the ones who experienced that event were equally impressed with its gravity, and I've given some thought to what it might have meant to them. We have to take into account that these were Hebraic disciples with a knowledge of their recorded history with God. So they would have considered the ongoing story of the heavens and the earth when they pondered what happened. With that in mind, here are some things they might have been thinking when their persons were filled with God's Spirit.

To make my first point, I have to give a little recent history. I was raised, predominantly, in traditional evangelical churches. While I was in college, I started having encounters with the Lord that led me to more charismatic churches. To someone who was used to singing three hymns, passing the offering plate, and listening to a sermon, the charismatic church services seemed downright lively. The music was contemporary and there were actual demonstrations of the Holy Spirit's power. I heard accurate prophecies, watched people get healed, and heard believers speak in tongues. And I learned in those years how much the day of Pentecost applied to me. I was taught that the free gift of the Spirit was for me, too, and that I could experience everything I read about in the Bible. So, I received the Holy Spirit, and started a wonderful, supernatural journey. I learned all about the gifts of the Spirit, and nowadays it would not seem strange to me at all if someone came up and said, "Hey Christopher, I've got a prophetic word for you."

In the years since my own personal awakening, I've visited many Spirit-filled congregations, participated in revivals, and observed and operated in many Holy Spirit manifestations. But here's where I'm not sure our understanding of the gift of the Holy Spirit is the same as those who first experienced that blessing: Follow my train of thought for a minute. Most of our understanding of the Holy Spirit is as an advent of power. In other words, when the Holy Spirit fell on the believers, it opened the door for us to do all the things Jesus was doing. So now we can all prophesy... And now we can heal people... and so on... I could sum up all the teaching I've heard on the Holy Spirit in this category — It gave us power to do the impossible. However, I'm convinced that's not what the disciples were thinking in the upper room. Here's why: They were already doing those things prior to the day of Pentecost.

In the gospels Jesus sends the disciples out with instructions to heal the sick, raise the dead, and cast out devils. And they did. They even came back to Jesus rejoicing because the evil spirits obeyed them. So I have a hard time thinking the newly empowered disciples would have thought, "Oh, now we can go out and do miracles." They had already been doing those things for years as they walked around with Jesus. So to them, this day was about something else entirely. Now, here's a disclaimer: I'm not saying that Pentecost wasn't about giving us power to heal the sick and prophesy. It did do that in abundance. However, that could not have been the primary thought running through the disciples' minds when the wind rushed through the room. If it had just been about miraculous gifts, that wouldn't have been much of a change — more like a continuation of what they were already experiencing. So what did they think was happening?

That answer lies in the first outward miracle they observed on the day of Pentecost. As soon as they were filled with the Spirit, the disciples began to speak "with other tongues." And as a big crowd gathered, people from all different nationalities and languages listened in. To their surprise, everyone could understand what was being said. The language barrier had disappeared. God doesn't do anything by accident. So there was a very big reason He chose this day to reverse a condition that had been around for over 2,000 years. This was God saying, "I'm lifting the curse of the tower of Babel." Now why would He have lifted the language barrier unless He was also saying, "And, by the way, what you were trying to do at Babel, I'm now giving you full permission to pursue"?

Follow the story arc from *Genesis* to *Acts*. Mankind tried to access the heavenly realms – but they weren't ready for it. So God put a stop to it by confusing the language. Over time, God finished telling the redemption story, culminating in the actions of His Son, Jesus. Then Jesus promised to fill believers with the Holy Spirit, thereby putting something incorruptible and holy inside each disciple. Finally, on Pentecost, the Holy Spirit descended and made it possible for believers to access the heavenly realms — safely and purely. In an act of punctuation, God removed the language barrier He used to keep them out of heaven because it was no longer needed. To anyone paying attention, this was the end of the (very long!)

sentence the Father started speaking at the tower of Babel. That sentence was all about accessing the heavenly realms.

If you're wondering what changed to make this all possible, we need to go back a few chapters. If you will recall, we talked about Heaven being off-limits to the sinful. It's that same principle we mentioned about corrupted, perishing things not being able to access the incorruptible, non-perishing realms. Once the Holy Spirit came to dwell in the believers, a part of them was no longer perishing. Their spirit had been infused with the Holy Spirit, meaning that at least part of them was able to ascend to the courts of the Lord. Again, going back to the first chapter, that's why we talk about going to heaven "in the Spirit." That's why John's journey, recorded in the book of *Revelation,* occurred "in the Spirit." That is the state in which we have access to the highest heavens. That is why it was safe for the Father to open the door to heaven and invite us in. Simply put, because of Pentecost, our spirits are able to handle the journey.

There's one more clue in *Acts, chapter 2,* that the day of Pentecost was all about an entrance to the heavenly realms. It's the "tongues of fire" which came to rest on each believer in the room. Let's think about the Hebraic history of the disciples that day. When they saw a shoot of flame over them, what image would that have conjured up? Might they have thought back to a very large "tongue of fire" that held a special place in their history? Do you think it would have reminded them of the pillar of fire that guided Israel through the desert and rested over the tabernacle?

I don't think this is too much of a poetic license here; I believe the tongues of fire above each believer were likely the same phenomenon observed above the tabernacle — only in individual form. And, if you've been following the relationship between the pillar of fire and a connection to heaven, then we might make the following conclusion: On the day of Pentecost, the Lord gave every believer an individual tower to the heavens. That means you.

CHAPTER 22

OPENING YOUR EYES

A big part of our ministry, Dwelling Place, is conducting workshops to help people realize their own access to the heavenly realms. I try to include as many hands-on activities as possible because nothing is as effective as actual, first-hand experience. Over the years, I've honed in on some exercises that help people get past the greatest obstacle in this process: The belief that it's hard! In other words, the hardest part is realizing it's not that hard. So the exercises we're going to cover in this chapter are designed to take all of the struggle out of this endeavor. As hard as it is to wrap your mind around it, we were made to experience heaven. Also, as we saw in the last chapter, the way has been opened before us, so all we need to do is go in. Keep in mind as we get started that these are the basics. Once these processes become comfortable to you, the experience will take on a life of its own. The Lord is always ready to reveal more of Himself to those who want to see, so once you get started, the sky's the limit (well... not really).

First, this will go smoother if you're in a quiet place and you have a few minutes to spare. I'm not saying to skip this if you're in a rush; but to go through it step-by-step you might need to block off some time. The first thing I want you to do is imagine a restful and peaceful place. It can be somewhere you've been before, or something completely imagined. For the next few minutes, paint that picture, whatever it may be, in your mind. Fill in all the details you like in your imagination. Then, just look at it for a minute or two before you go on to the next paragraph.

Most everyone likes to imagine an idyllic setting where they can take a few deep breaths and take it easy. And normally it's not too hard to use your imagination in that capacity. So here's a big tip for you as keep going: Everything you see in the heavenly realms, you will see just like that — with your imagination. However, as soon as I bring up that word — imagination — that causes a bit of a stir. Some people might think, "Well, if it's just my imagination, then is this worth doing?" Most of that is an ingrained response to our years of institutional education. Notice that the imagination is tolerated in preschool and kindergarten, and then practically shunned as you get older. I'm sure that plays into the hands of the fallen angels perfectly. They would love it if whole societies drilled the value of the imagination out of its citizens, because they know it can be a powerful tool. Your imagination is your link to all things unseen. You just experienced its capacity when you imagined a peaceful place. In that moment, you were seeing things that weren't in the earthly realm. You were seeing unseen things. That's why God gave you your imagination in the first place.

The imagination is the "eyes of your heart" that the Apostle Paul spoke of in the letter to the Ephesians. Remember, Paul prayed that those heart-eyes would be enlightened. In a sense, that's what we're practicing in this chapter. We're working on getting the eyes of your heart (your imagination) focused on the Holy Spirit. We need to get comfortable treating it like the powerful tool that it is. Even the word itself has a dynamic meaning. Here's its definition from the Merriam-Webster dictionary:

"The act or power of forming a mental image of something not present to the senses or never before wholly perceived in reality."

Or to put it in my own words:

"The act of seeing something that's not necessarily in the earthly dimension."

One last tip before we go on to the next step. You may find yourself struggling with your imagination because you think you're just making it all up. That's a valid feeling in this process, and I can almost guarantee that you'll feel that way at some point. Here's the strange truth about that. The part of you that is generating the images just happens to be the part of you that's been filled with the Holy Spirit. Remember, the Holy Spirit is inside of you now. So yes, there is a part of you that's "making it up." I tell people as they begin exploring this reality that if you're waiting and waiting for some image to slap you on the side of your head as it descends from the heavens, you are going to be very frustrated. All of this will come from the Holy Spirit within you. That means it will feel like it's coming from the inside, not the outside. That doesn't make it less of an experience at all. In fact, it should validate this whole process because it confirms the Source. So give your imagination some room to work. Don't just write it off as being a silly part of your being. It's the tool God gave you to see the unseen. And if you're worried about being "safe" in imaging any of this, you can do what one of my colleagues did in order to "free up" her conscience and know that she was in keeping with God's will and not her own: Just verbally "cover" your imagination with the Blood of Jesus. Or say whatever you need to say, or request in prayer whatever you need to, in order to ensure you're on the right track while you proceed. Assuming you've done that or whatever else (if anything) the Holy Spirit leads you to do, let's start putting it to work.

If you're still in that quiet place, try doing this: Close your eyes and imagine the room you are sitting in. See it exactly as it exists in your earthly reality. With those internal eyes, scan the whole picture to make sure you have every piece of furniture, every decoration, and every color just like you see it with your biological eyes. Take as long as you need to do this, and simply build the picture like you did before. When you're done, read the next paragraph.

*   *   *

As you use the eyes of your heart, try to describe out-loud what you're seeing. If you literally can't verbalize it for some reason, don't let that stop you from going forward in this experience. (I make a good point for the importance of this verbalization in the next chapter, however.) But back to the exercise, as you're building the picture of the room, verbalize each detail as you see it, as if you're reporting to someone sitting there with you. So with your eyes closed you might be saying, "Okay, now I see the couch I'm sitting on, and over there is the lamp. I can see the fireplace and the pictures on the far wall... " Throughout this whole process, keep reminding yourself to verbalize as much as possible.

Now do the first step again and once you see the room in your imagination, ask the Lord, out-loud, to show you where He is in the room. Then without over thinking or processing, go with the very first impression of where you imagine Him to be in the room. Don't worry about if you're right or wrong, just take a guess. Then take note of where He is and open your eyes to read the next step.

Next we're going to start looking at Jesus, wherever He might be in your picture. So go right back to imagining the room with Jesus in it, and then focus on the following details: What kind of clothes is He wearing? Are there any colors you can see on His person or garment? What is His expression? You can take as much time as you need on each area, but just remember to take a guess. Don't wait until you're seeing everything in perfect focus and clarity. Simply go with your impressions. Most people, when they do this for the first time, are insecure about their answers, but there's no need to be. Start with His clothes: What's your first guess of how He's dressed? Nothing is too silly or outlandish; so don't over-think it. Go back to the picture now, and when you've filled in some of the blanks, feel free to keep going.

Did you remember to take some guesses? And did you remember to keep verbalizing everything out loud (if you can or feel you should)? If it's going well, then let's take a few more steps. The next time you go back to imagining the room and Jesus, get close to Him. For some readers, you might already be close to Him. He might be sitting next to you on the couch, for instance. But others might have seen Him standing in the far corner of the room. If that's you, don't worry.

Remember, there isn't a "right" way to see this. Take the next few minutes and go back to the picture. Then ask the Lord to come near to you. Or, if you prefer, you can get close to Him. All you need to do is simply imagine yourself moving closer to Him. You can watch yourself get up off the couch and close the distance until you are near enough to touch. If you would rather ask Him to do it that's fine, too. Ask Him, out loud, if He wouldn't mind coming over to where you are, and then go with the first impressions of what He did. Again, try not to put the images through a mental filter. Just go with your best guess and keep moving through the steps.

Now that's He's close to you, take another look at Him like you did before. What is your impression of His face? What's His expression? Is He doing anything with His hands? What's His posture? Look at those things, and then verbalize what you see as if someone was in the room with you. Then while you're sitting close together, look at Him directly and ask the following question: "What do you like about me?" Try your best not to filter the thoughts that come into your head, but go with the first things you imagine Him saying to you in response to your question. It's okay if all this seems strange or if you have a problem with it – we'll do some troubleshooting in the next chapter. Once you've listened to Him tell you a few things, ask Him why He loves you or what He thinks about you. Don't filter this experience through your worthiness in your own human eyes. Just do your best to sit still and let Him give you some of His affection. Remember, He can speak to you in many ways: He may use words, images, phrases… When you're done, open your eyes again and finish this chapter.

It can be a wonderful experience to have a sit-down

conversation with your Lord. As we talked about in the intro-duction, Jesus promised His disciples that something just as good as sitting around the table with Him was available through the Holy Spirit. Therefore, we should be able to see Him and talk with Him as much as we like. It's all part of the advantage of the Holy Spirit. Anyone who wants to take the time to culti-vate a life in the heavens can start with these exercises. If these aren't working, try some others listed in the "Different Ways to Look" chapter. Or ask the Holy Spirit to direct you. Ask Jesus for ideas… The point is to come into His presence in a new way.

Listening to His encouragement and learning to sit and talk with Him is a crucial part of this process, so don't rush it. Take your time. Take weeks if you need to. And when you feel like it's getting a little more normal and a little easier, go on to the next exercises. Before we do that, though, we'll take a look at some troubleshooting tips, just in case you get stuck.

Chapter 23

Troubleshooting

I hope you've never had a serious injury that required a long rehabilitation, but you're probably familiar with the process. When something in your body is in really bad shape, you have to gradually work it back to health and strength. If the injury is very serious, and the affected muscles aren't used for a long time, they go into a state of atrophy. When that happens, the road to recovery starts very slowly — because getting atrophied muscles to move in a full range of motion can be a challenge. Therefore, the primary concern is to get it to back to its basic functions. Only after that do you begin applying pressure and exercises to build up strength.

It's okay to think of the eyes of your heart in the same way. They haven't suffered an injury, but they might be in a state of atrophy, maybe from lack of use. Therefore, we should treat these exercises like rehabilitation. Don't worry about lifting one-hundred pounds right off the bat. We need to start slowly; and before you know it, this spiritual muscle will be able to do things you never dreamed possible. However, in the beginning most people have a little frustration.

One of the most common complaints I hear is that the picture isn't clear. I'm told things like, "When I tried to look at Jesus, all I could see was a fuzzy face. I couldn't make out any features." Or, sometimes I hear, "Christopher, I just don't see a well as you do." My response to this is always be patient and practice, practice, practice. If you want the muscle to work and be strong, you have to be committed to the rehab.

When I started taking trips to heaven, it was the easiest thing I had ever done — for the first few weeks. Then it got hard. The advice and exercises you've been reading about were born out of those weeks and months of frustrating effort. I stuck with it because I was hooked from the start. I knew, from the very first trip, that I had waited my whole life to experience a connection to the heavenly dimension — so there was no way I was going to back out just because it got hard. At the end of those months of rehab, I learned the lesson I shared with you in the last chapter — this isn't that hard. I have a knack for making spiritual things way too hard. I always think there are rules I'm going to break or that there's some way I'll find to mess it all up. But in the end, I found out what I'm sharing with you; that God didn't make a bunch of hoops for us to jump through. We just need to believe, and He does the rest. I shared all of that to give you hope if you're struggling. Even if it takes a few months of learning to let go and trust the Holy Spirit, have courage. It took me some time, too.

What I've been sharing with you is easy and accessible to everyone. However, that doesn't mean it won't take commitment. Even if you can just barely make out the person of Jesus sitting in the room with you, that's okay. Give it time. Before you know it, the eyes of your heart will get strong and you'll see things in great detail. For me, I noticed how far I had come after almost two years of heavenly journeys. It happened when I took my glasses off and began to walk down a hallway. Just so you'll know, without my glasses, I can't function. I can't drive, see a television, read a book, or make out the features on someone's face if they're standing more than four feet away. But when I stopped halfway down the hall and looked around, I noticed something with my uncorrected eyes. I could make out the vague shape of pictures hanging on the wall and I could see the lights in the ceiling. It was all fuzzy, just like I expected it to be. Then I realized I could see more detail in the Spirit than I could with my biological eyes. I had never thought to make a comparison; but without corrective lenses, it was a no-contest. The eyes of my heart actually worked better than the eyes on my face. However, that was only after years of doing this. If that's what you desire, too, then be prepared to practice.

Now, let's say you're doing those exercises, but you get stuck when you start talking with Jesus. For instance, what if you ask Him the questions I mentioned, but you can't seem to hear Him say anything in return? My advice here is to loosen up a little and take a guess. It's okay, especially early on, to let your imagination do the work. Ask Him again, out-loud, to tell you something He likes about you. Then go with the very first word or phrase or image that pops into your head. Remember, nothing is too silly. If Jesus says He likes your goofy looking ears (this has happened, by the way) then re-ceive that and ask Him to tell you something else. Part of our difficulty is that we try to be so serious, as if we're afraid of offending God with our impropriety. Try loosening up and taking some of the pressure off. You have your whole life to do this, so take time to have a light conversation with Jesus. He might even use humor or something very unex-pected to help you relax or to break through your barriers.

If you're still having trouble hearing Him talk to you,

focus a bit more on your imagination. When you ask Him the questions, what do you imagine He would say to you? As you can probably tell, all of these techniques are to get you to loosen up so that the Holy Spirit can start speaking from within you. Sometimes this is a big leap of faith and you might find yourself thinking, "I'm afraid I'm going to make Jesus say whatever I want Him to say. Since it's my imagination, how do I know I'm imagining it right?" That's a great question to ask — and a normal one. However, it might reveal another thing we think about the Holy Spirit that is totally in error. It's hard to admit, but a lot of folks think that the Holy Spirit is very small and very weak. If you get trapped into that worry, ask yourself if you can actually make Jesus do anything!? Does that help you put it into perspective?

Here's what I mean by that all that: If we think that we're controlling the whole experience, simply because we are using the God-given gift of the imagination, then we are making a big statement about the Holy Spirit's power. It's a belief that our intellect and our will is stronger than His, and that there is no way the Holy Spirit could override our powerful minds. It's a subtle way of saying that we are stronger and more powerful than the Holy Spirit! However, isn't it far more reasonable to think that God will honor your desire to get to know Him? Isn't it more "correct" to view the Holy Spirit as a totally dynamic entity who can seamlessly co-labor with your imagination? The Holy Spirit is an actual part of the Almighty. I'm confident our intellect doesn't trump His power. Therefore, don't fall into that trap of thinking your mind is too much for Him to handle.

Finally, you might have encountered another hurdle in this process — fatigue. Many people who try these exercises feel exhausted after ten or fifteen minutes. All I can tell you is that it's normal and that it's another proof that you are rehabilitating the eyes of your heart. It's going to take some time to build up endurance. With practice, you'll be able to spend hours in the heavenly realms.

CHAPTER 24

DIFFERENT WAYS TO LOOK

Here's something to try the next time you're in the car. Do the exact same exercise I mentioned before (but make sure to keep your eyes open!)… Just look around the car and ask the Lord, out-loud, to show you where He is. Then, verbalize (or at least picture or think) the very first place you imagined Him to be. When you think about it, we all know God is everywhere. The fancy word for that is "omnipresent." So of course He's in the car with you. All you're doing is letting the Holy Spirit show you what's going on in the unseen realms. Now once you found Him, take some guesses about the details like you did before. How is He dressed? What is His expression? Is He doing anything? Then ask Him some questions like, "What do you like about me? What is something that You really want me to know today? What is something I need to know tomorrow?"

This is just another way to work on interacting with Him as a person and not a distant deity that you have to call on a very long-distance prayer line. It's supposed to be closer and more intimate than that. Also, the Lord is delighted when people come in close to Him and treat Him with familiarity and affection, so don't worry about being informal. He is far more concerned that you know Him for who He really is than if you're showing the right amount of respect and propriety.

I suggest having these conversations in the Spirit as

often as possible, especially if they're unplanned. Sometimes you can catch yourself by surprise; and before you know it, you've been talking with Jesus the entire time you were washing the dishes or something. Just make sure to watch Him and relate to Him like you would anyone else in the room. If you've been talking for a while, take a break and see what's on His mind. All you have to do is ask Him and then trust those first impressions in your imagination.

Here's one more thing to try; but for this one you probably want to be at home and in a quiet place. Go through the whole introductory exercise. Imagine the room just like it is. Find Jesus in the room. Look at some of the details and begin a basic conversation. Then, when there's a break in the conversation, ask the Lord to take you to the Garden. As soon as you ask Him, verbalize the first things you see Him doing. You might say something like, "Okay, Lord, I just saw you get up and take my hands. Now I see you leading me out the door..." Whatever you imagined, talk it out as if you're reporting it to someone.

I brought up the Garden because it seems to be a natural place to visit first. (But it's okay if that's not the first place He shows you — this is a suggestion.) It's important to know that some things in that environment will look familiar and some might not. People have reported seeing colors differently, talking to animals, and even flying. None of that is off-limits in the Garden. If at any point you get confused, take a deep breath and find Jesus. If you don't know where He went, ask the Lord to show you — just like you did in the first exercises. Also, if you get concerned that you're doing it all wrong, just stop and ask Jesus how you're doing. He'll tell you if you need to do something different. Even if you totally blank out and loose the whole experience (and that does happen), try taking a short break. When you're ready, close your eyes and go back to the last thing you saw clearly. You can use your memory to build the picture as you remember seeing it. Then find Jesus in the picture and stay close to Him. And if nothing seems to be working, go back to the basics. I don't know about you, but I think it's a joy to sit and talk with Jesus in any environment, my living room included.

That brings me to the most helpful tip of all: Whatever you do and wherever you go, keep looking at Jesus. If He takes you somewhere, stay right next to Him. If you go off exploring the Garden, ask Him to stay right next to you. Periodically, glance at Him and see what He's doing. Take in some of the details of His expression. Ask Him if there's something He wants to show you in His Garden. His presence will be all the help you need in this process. And remember, there is not a "right" and "wrong" Jesus encounter! If your journey begins differently, remember that Jesus knows what you need and how to meet you. Trust that.

As you walk and talk with Him, there's no telling what will happen. He may take you on an adventure into the heavenly realms, or He might want to sit and talk for a while. I've experienced both, and sometimes I've had whole seasons of one or the other. I think He knows what's best for us, even if we have other plans.

In these last chapters, you might have noticed I keep using the phrase "out-loud." No, I'm not trying to make people give you strange looks while you talk to yourself (although that might happen). In my experience, talking out loud helps you focus. It's such a big help, but it doesn't come naturally to some folks, so I sound like a broken record when I'm teaching the basics. On a biological level, there is a part of your brain that responds to your own, spoken voice; so hearing yourself talk — about anything — is very important. That's why some self-affirmation like, "You can do this, Christopher," is so effective. It's also why speaking negative things about yourself can lead to a destructive cycle. The Bible says that life and death is in the power of the tongue (*Proverbs 18:21*), so putting it to work while you use the eyes of your heart is a helpful combination.

CHAPTER 25

MORE EXPERIENCES

Once I was with a small group, helping them with the introductory exercises. Everyone was taking turns reporting what they were seeing, but one lady in particular, who was going through a terribly difficult time in her life, felt really "blocked" at first. She kept seeing nothing but "black" and hearing nothing at all. Finally, a faint image appeared in her mind's eye as they say. It was a particular type of bird. There was nothing else, no elaborate setting, etc. When she saw that image but was still feeling "blank," I asked her what was lovely about that bird and she was able to name a few attributes which spoke to her heart, as the tears that began to fall down her face testified. Despite the tears, she immediately felt much better. Later, a friend looked up some Christian symbols of that particular bird — and what she read was exactly in keeping with her particular situation and it showed her just what Jesus thought of her valiant efforts. That image continued speaking to her in different ways for weeks, helping her through a very rough time.

Sometimes when it's hard to see or hear anything, you just have to trust what the Lord is showing you and build on that. It's a good reminder to be patient and trust the impressions you're getting, even if it's not quite what you expected. In fact, one of the best exercises you can do on your own is something I call the blank slate. Instead of seeing Jesus in the Garden, or in the room you're in, try starting from scratch. Sit quietly and turn your heart to the Lord and then see what pops up in the eyes of your heart. Make sure to go with the first impressions no matter how bizarre it may seem. Some of my most memorable experiences have started by letting go of all my expectations and trusting the first things the Holy Spirit shows me.

For instance, on one occasion the first thing I saw was a train. It was an old style steam engine, the kind I only know from books and movies. I was tempted to write it off as my mind playing tricks on me, but I took a step of faith and acknowledged that I did indeed see a train. I walked up to the platform as if to get on, but I noticed to my left there was a map of all the stops this particular train was going to make. My eyes focused on the stop called "The Park." When I got on the train, it started to chug slowly forward, gaining speed. I rode it for a few minutes, wondering the whole time if I did the right thing by just going with the first images that the eyes of my heart could discern. Then, the train started to climb up a hill. The slope kept getting steeper and steeper until it was almost vertical. Just when I thought the train would fall off the tracks, it took off into the sky and eventually into the cosmos.

I kept looking through the window at the cosmic view, and I noticed the train was coming to a stop. I decided to get off and see where I was and, sure enough, I stepped onto a platform fronting a beautiful park. I walked to the entrance and found Jesus waiting for me with His big, accepting smile, and we spent the rest of the day walking and talking along the walkways. It turned out to be a great adventure, but I might have missed it if I thought seeing an old steam locomotive was somehow off-limits or not spiritual enough to bother with. Remember that if you ever get stuck or want to try the blank slate exercise.

On a different note, here's an example of another friend of mine who wanted to go to the heavenlies on behalf of her loved one. She imagined Jesus approaching her with a white box. Then, she imagined herself and Jesus going to that person and handing over the box. Before she knew it, the vision unfolded before her like a movie and she found herself leaning in, interestedly, while the person in question opened the gift in front of a smiling Jesus. The person pulled out a number of seemingly unrelated objects, but my friend remembered each one, and later shared that vision and the objects with her loved one.

As you can imagine, each and every object had a deep, personal meaning. Again, you have to let go and trust what you're seeing. Her first impression was that the objects were unrelated, and they didn't make sense to her. As it turned out, the Holy Spirit was leading the whole time. This is a great idea for anyone who would like to bless someone while they are in the Spirit. Ask Jesus if He has a gift for them (and He always does) and then see what's inside. Then, ask Jesus if He wants you to share it with them, or just keep it tucked away in your heart until they can see it for themselves.

Lastly, I'd like to tell you about a time when a friend wanted to join me on a heavenly visit. He met me at my office and decided he would follow me in the Spirit wherever I was going that day. I made sure to describe everything out loud so that he could follow along. As I spoke what I was seeing, he imagined himself in the same picture with me. We eventually came to a courtyard in the middle of three heavenly buildings. I could see that they were white, and that the largest one had an interesting roofline. It had three domes, with the center dome being the largest. However, I didn't mention any of this to my friend. I just described the courtyard and told him that we were surrounded by buildings. I told him to look around for himself and then report back to me what he saw. After a few minutes, my friend says, "I see three white buildings, and the big one has a domed roofline. It's like three domes and the one in the middle is higher than the others." I was shocked when I heard this, because I never knew I could go to heaven with other people and we would all see the same things! After I got over the surprise, we both walked into the building we recognized and had a wonderful meeting with the Father.

These are just a few examples of what's possible, and I hope it gives you the sense of how limitless these adventures can be. The door is open for everyone, so don't be afraid to have your own, personalized experience. Even if it doesn't look like what I've described, just give it a try and keep your focus on Jesus.

Chapter 26

Loose Ends

There is so much about our world that is designed to keep people focused on the temporal things of the earth. God isn't the one doing that. We've already talked about the spiritual forces of wickedness intent on keeping you out of the heavens. I also mentioned you might feel some opposition when you start looking up. Between the fallen angels, and the fact that you are rehabilitating a spiritual muscle, you might feel like a journey into the unseen reality is not worth it. I'm not going to try to convince you to do it, but I will reiterate what makes it so rewarding — discovering the Lord. It's what keeps me focused on the heavenly realms. Not the things I've seen or the places I've visited.

I've seen people get excited about all the peripheral issues, and sometimes they pursue their access to heaven for all the wrong reasons. They want to see the heavenly palaces or meet the angels, and they want it to happen right away. In my experience, those folks never last. Once they experience the more "sensational" things, they quickly loose interest and go after the next phenomenon that looks enticing. Their interest falls away because they never got into the true blessing being offered. It's not in the places you visit — it's Who you are visiting them with.

In every aspect of life, the primary issue will always be your relationship to the Lord. If you recall, I spent years getting to know Jesus in the Spirit. Sure, we visited different places, but it was always a way for Him to reveal Himself a little bit more. It was only after building that foundation that He introduced me to angels that I could count as friends. By the time that started happening, I was already convinced that the greatest blessing in the heavens was knowing the One who made them.

I encourage you to check your own motivation as you practice looking into the heavens. If you'll stay focused on the Lord, then you can have a life-long discovery of a realm you were purposed to live in.

Chapter 27

At Home

We moved around a lot as I was growing up. I think on average we stayed in each place about three years. That amounts to six different homes before I left for college, and there are parts of moving I remember fondly and some I don't. On the positive side, moving so much made me very adaptable, willing to try new things, and a natural traveler. Another helpful side-effect was the ability to pack up and move a house. My mother could box up all our possessions and have them on a moving truck in twenty-four hours; and I pride myself on continuing her expertise in that area. Also, it was always fun choosing the new house, and a few times I even got to ride around with mom and dad while a realtor took us on the parade of homes.

Then there were the challenges: It was always hard to be the new kid. I had to make friends and sort out a whole new school system, and it seemed everyone around me had the benefit of being there their whole life. That made for a challenging social disadvantage. When you're a kid and you're told you're going to uproot everything and start over, you feel a lot of different things, mostly some instability. But when you arrive at the new house and your stuff is set up in your new room, the sense of permanence comes back. You know that even though you are still in a daunting transition, you can go back to your room, surrounded by your own things, and feel settled. In between leaving the old place and getting moved into the new one, you feel like a wanderer. Somehow, all of that fades away when you're holding the key to your new home. Even if it's a totally unknown environment outside, it all looks the same on the inside.

For a good two years I had wandered around heaven, visiting other peoples homes. I had seen throne rooms, governmental palaces, and angelic mansions. One day, I was invited to go see yet another heavenly palace. My heavenly Dad, Uriel, and Breanadan accompanied me that day, and they brought me to a wide, green plain with mountains on the left and an ocean on the right. There was a steep drop-off, like a cliff face, where the grassy field met the ocean on the right. I could see a river that ran across the entire landscape. It started in the mountains on the left, and it cascaded down in beautiful waterfalls before settling into a lazy flow. The river meandered through the fields in front of me before spilling over the cliff face in a long, continuous waterfall, down into the ocean below.

A bridge crossed the river in the middle of the plain, and on the other side stood a palace I had never seen before. It was bright and angular, much like Uriel's home, but the waterfalls and lush green colors reminded me of Gabriel's home as well. I turned to Breanadan and asked, "Whose home is this?" He responded, "It's yours." We walked over the bridge and into a dwelling place that seemed more extravagant than anything I would have thought I deserved. Getting more (or better) than I deserve is a running theme with me in the Spirit. Isn't God's grace and generosity wonderful and encouraging? They took me on a tour just like a realtor would when showing a house, and I was hooked from the first entryway. Everything about it seemed perfectly suited to me, and even though it was huge and palatial, it fit like a glove. As my angelic friends walked me around my heavenly home, they pointed out each feature like proud craftsmen. They knew how much I would like it, and they were happy to tell me which parts they had designed.

As I explored the palace I kept a mental map of the place, and I even attempted to draw it out on paper like an architectural schematic to keep track of what I was discovering. Over time, I learned to navigate its hallways and rooms like I would any building on earth, and that made it even easier to be there. I figured if the Lord saw fit to show me my dwelling place in the heavens, I ought to get to know it like the back of my hand.

For a while there were no other palaces to visit and no new angelic friends to meet. It was a time for me to get settled in my home, and every morning I would start my day in this wonderful place. In my earthly body, I would go up to my office over the garage, sit down with a cup of tea and close my natural eyes. In the Spirit, I would find myself walking among the familiar halls and meeting rooms of my heavenly palace — or one of my other favorite spots – the garden. By the west wing of the palace was a lush garden filled with plants of every variety. In the center was a white pavilion that seemed like the perfect place to meet someone before taking a walk through the manicured flora. It was my morning routine to meet up with my heavenly Dad at the pavilion and walk and talk the morning away. We would stroll around, my good friend Arnol perched on my shoulder, and discuss whatever was on our minds.

Every day I spent learning to live in my heavenly home, the more I became convinced I belonged there. Do you remember the scripture about being a "citizen of heaven" (*Philippians 3:20*)? At this point in my journey, that was becoming a reality.

Being in heaven was growing on me, and the added stability of my home made it easier to spend more time up there. But there was a bigger point the Lord was making in all of this. Take a look at something Jesus said about our heavenly residence:

> *In My Father's house are many dwelling places; if it were not so, I would have told you; for I go to prepare a place for you. If I go and prepare a place for you, I will come again and receive you to Myself, that where I am, there you may be also. And you know the way where I am going." (John 14: 2-4)*

For the last 2,000 years, Jesus has been in the heavenly dimension preparing places for all of us, just like the one given to me. He makes it pretty clear to His disciples what He will be working on after He leaves the earth realm. That makes me wonder about something. Did the Lord introduce me to my heavenly home because His project is almost finished and He's ready to start revealing what He's been working on for two millennia? Could this be an indication that we are at the door of a very big transition? Notice what comes right after Jesus gets the houses ready:

> *I will come again and receive you to Myself, that where I am, there you may be also.*

CHAPTER 28

TRANSITIONS

I want you to imagine that you are one of Jesus' disciples during the time of His earthly ministry. Do your best to think about what life must have been like as you traveled around with Him. Maybe you were one of the people that left everything to follow Him; or maybe you can see yourself as one of the twelve apostles. Imagine actually being there when He changed water to wine or fed the multitude. No matter what you thought you knew about the laws that govern reality, you might have re-thought some things as you watched Him do miracle after miracle on His way to the cross. Now imagine you were around after He had risen, when He entered the room in His resurrected body. You would have been looking at a dead man, only He was clearly alive — and He got an upgrade. Finally, imagine you were on the mountain when He ascended.

In that moment, the man you had personally known for three years suddenly begins to float up into the sky and into another dimension. If you had been there for that, you might think about heaven very differently than we do today. For us, heaven is a spiritual conversation. For them, heaven was a known physical dimension. Think about it another way: If one of your best friends took you on a hike through the woods and, when no one was looking, showed you that he could phase out of this dimension and enter into another, would you think something spiritual had just happened and not something physical — despite the fact that he visibly vanished and reappeared? Probably not. You would have come face-to-face with a physical space that is every bit as real and present as the one you knew as "earth" but didn't operate "normally" as you were used to. This can be tough to wrap your mind around, so let's look at it one other way.

Spiritual conversations are rarely about defined, physical dimensions. They cover things like joy, inner peace, the health of your prayer life, or finding your purpose. Or they could be about sin and redemption or receiving salvation. For something to be considered spiritual, it has to be about the inner, non-physical parts of your life. I'm certainly making a generality here, and there are aspects of our spiritual life that influence physical things. Supernatural healing is one example that doesn't fit into the box. However, I think the general point can hold water. In our everyday speech and thought, spiritual things are in a different category from physical things.

For instance, we use a certain type of speech to explain how an airplane flies or how the microwave works, because they have physical properties. Personally, I've never heard someone give me a spiritual reason for either of those. Conversely, no one has ever offered a physical explanation of heaven, and I think that's where we've become different from the disciples who observed the existance of another physical dimension. They got to watch Jesus become trans-dimensional — in His physcial body. That changes things. After observing that event, you would have never spoken of heaven as a spiritual concept. It would have been understood as a physical reality. We think in terms of spiritual verses physical, with subjects being relegated to either category. That's a habit we must break if we hope to see things the way the disciples did.

Let me throw one more log on the fire before we make some conclusions. Jesus was one of three people in the Bible to become trans-dimensional. Enoch was first, followed by Elijah, and then finally Jesus. These three men, in their physical bodies, went to the other physical dimension we call heaven. But that's not the end of the story. If you read the descriptions of Jesus' future return to the earth realm, we will see that others will make this very same transition. Take a look at this:

> For this we say to you by the word of the Lord, that we who are alive and remain until the coming of the Lord, will not precede those who have fallen asleep. For the Lord Himself will descend from heaven with a shout, with the voice of the archangel and with the trumpet of God, and the dead in Christ will rise first. Then we who are alive and remain will be caught up together with them in the clouds to meet the Lord in the air, and so we shall always be with the Lord. (1 Thessalonians 4: 15-17)

Everyone who's alive when Jesus comes back gets some special treatment. They don't have to die, and they get an instant translation into their heavenly form. In other words, a whole generation of people will have an Enoch experience. Some years ago, I had a conversation with the Lord about this. I spoke of it in detail in *Caught Up in the Spirit*. The point I'd like to recal here is that the last generation of Christians will be a last generation of Enochs. Enoch walked with God for three-hundred years before He made a final visit to the heavenly dimension and stayed there. It is my opinion that he spent those three centuries walking in and out of the heavenly dimesnion until one day it was more natural for him to be there instead of here. I expect the last generation of Christians to do the same thing, only in less time. Because we have the Holy Spirit, we are more equipped than Enoch to discover the heavenly dimension and learn to live there. When Jesus returns, I expect He will find a whole group of believers that have already walked and talked with Him in the heavens. Dare I say they will have already done it in their bodies? There is a prescedent for this. We have our three historical examples and a prophetic promise that applies to everyone in a given moment of time. So this is not a question of possibility. Now, let's try to bring some things together:

- Jesus said He was going to prepare places for us in the other dimension.
- When those places are finished, He said He's coming back to get us and take us there.
- When He comes back, there is a whole generation of people waiting for Him that have already become familiar with transitioning between the dimensions.
- That transition is as much a physical issue as it is a spiritual one.

With this in mind, consider my own experience of the heavenly dimension and how it's progressed in time. When it started, I was enjoying a newfound experience in the Spirit, but I had to find a quiet place with no disctractions in order to tune in at all. As the eyes of my heart got stronger, I could spend time in the heavenly places whenever I wanted, no matter what distractions were around me. In fact, I always thought it was kind of a challenge to keep focused on heaven while I was experiencing a loud or busy environment on earth. Also, the more I practiced, the more my other senses started to take part. At first, it was all seeing and hearing; but over time, touch, taste, and smell entered the experience. With each passing year, I could process more and more detail until my spiritual eyes worked better than my uncorrected, natural ones. Then, something changed again. I started to feel like more of me was making the trip. As I've said from the beginning, I knew I was experiencing things "in the Spirit," like the Apostle John did in the book of *Revelation*. But with time it felt like parts of my soul, and maybe even a few dozen cells of my body were going up, too.

The Apostle Paul had a heavenly experience that was so physcially present, he wondered if it was "in the body or out of the body" (*2 Corinthians 12: 2*). I can see why Paul had this question, because the line gets a little blurry sometimes. When I started to feel every step in the garden like I would the ground in my earthly back yard, I started thinking of this as more than "just" a spiritual experience. I don't think there are any easy ways to explain it, and I think that's why Paul couldn't figure it out either. Let's just say that over time, heaven becomes more than a concept. It even becomes more than a place you can sense and observe in the Spirit. Sooner or later, it becomes the place where you are.

There are many ways to experience heaven, and this book has focused almost entirely on doing so "in the Spirit." However, the more heaven is known, the more it will become known in every facet of reality — including physical. Therefore, for anyone looking to discover the heavenly realm, it cannot be thought of as only a spiritual experience. It isn't just an inward phenomenon. Sound strange? It wouldn't have to the disciples. Remember, they watched a man become trans-dimensional. Again, I urge you to imagine being there for that in order to get a sense of the physical reality of the heavenly realm. For Jesus, this was His last act on planet earth (until His return) and I believe that is on purpose. It is the end of a progression — the end of a road — that He had been traveling throughout His earthly sojourn. All that remains is for us to follow His example. Look back to Jesus' statements in *John 14* to see the invitation:

> *If I go and prepare a place for you, I will come again and receive you to Myself, that where I am, there you may be also. And you know the way where I am going." (John 14:3)*

Jesus said that we knew the way to where He was going, which of course prompted the disciples to ask for some clarification. Jesus gives them a profoundly simple answer. In the next verses, He says that He is the way. I hope by now I've made a good case for this experience being totally centered on Jesus, so I won't reiterate that. However, I do wonder if He's giving the Enoch generation a little wink and a nod when this is read. It's as if He's saying, "This is for all those believers who will prepare the way for My return. You know that I'm the way to the heavenly dimension. Feel free to start making the transition."

Therefore, if you're in that window of time that will see these things fullfilled, wouldn't you expect the knowledge of heaven and it's accessability to be on the rise? If you're standing at the door of this transition, shouldn't you start to see people beginning the Enoch process? If you will recall, we talked about how popular this subject has become in recent years. There are all kinds of books out right now that describe visits to heaven because it's simply just time for this revelation to come out. I would not be surprised if the emphasis on heaven is here — now — because the transition has started.

Finis

References:

Davies, Oliver and Thomas O'Loughlin. *Celtic Spirituality*. New York: Paulist Press, 1999.

Bamford, Christopher and William Parker Marsh. *Ecology and Holiness an anthology*. Aurora: Lindisfarne Books, 1987.

In the Palaces of Heaven

CPSIA information can be obtained
at www.ICGtesting.com
Printed in the USA
FFOW01n0038210114
3165FF